Instant Pot Cookbook

7 Different Cooking Methods with only 1 Device

Louis Laurent

CONTENTS

INTRODUCTION

Everyone wants to enjoy the home cooked meals they grew up with, but not all of us have the time or the culinary skills to replicate grandma's cooking. We find ourselves strapped for time and end up eating out constantly. Many of us have long lost the warmth of eating dinner as a family around the dinner table because modern life just isn't conducive to being stuck in the kitchen for more than 30 minutes max!

That's where the instant pot can help you restore that warmth and balance back into your life. The instant pot is a new generation of pressure cooker that can effectively cook 7 different ways! The versatility of a instant pot allows you to cook complex meals with ease and it even keeps the cleaning to a minimum as well.

This cookbook is going to open your eyes to the possibilities an instant pot can bring by proving everyday recipes you'll make regularly to more adventurous recipes you'll want to try out. The cookbook is categories by breakfast, chicken, beef, pork, seafood, vegetarian and dessert for ease of use.

Note: There are slight differences in the settings and modes between different instant pots. The design of the instant pot may influence how you decide to release pressure or the cooking time slightly. However the recipes in this book should be compatible with all types of instant pots.

BREAKFAST RECIPES

Poached Egg in Bell Pepper

INGREDIENTS

2 slices of whole wheat bread, toasted

2 slices of Smoked Mozerella

1 small bunch of Rucola

2 Fresh Eggs, refrigerated

2 Bell Peppers, ends cut off

Mock Hollandaise sauce:

⅔ cup mayonnaise

1½ teaspoons Dijon mustard

3 tablespoons orange juice

1 teaspoon fresh lemon juice

1 tablespoon white wine vinegar

½ teaspoons salt

1 teaspoon of Turmeric

INSTRUCTIONS

1. Make the mock Hollandaise sauce by whisking all of the ingredients together until smooth.
2. Prepare the instant pot by adding one cup of water and steamer basket (or trivet and steamer basket) and set aside.
3. Cut the bell pepper ends to form "cups" that are approximately 1.5" or 4cm high, and then break an egg inside of the cup. Cover with tin foil, and place in the steamer basket of the instant pot.
4. Close and lock the instant pot. Select the "low" pressure setting. When the pan reaches pressure, place the cooking time for 3-4 at low

pressure. When the cooking time is up, open the pressure cooker using the Normal Release method

5. Stack toast, smoked cheese, rucola, and pepper cups and cover with a generous dollop of mock-Hollandaise before serving.

Ham, Egg and Cheese Casserole

INGREDIENTS

32 ounce bag frozen cubed hash browns

1 large onion, diced

1-2 cups chopped ham

2 cups shredded cheddar cheese

10-12 large eggs

1 cup whole milk

1 teaspoon salt

1 teaspoon pepper

INSTRUCTIONS

1.	Spray the insert of a instant pot with nonstick cooking spray. Place ⅓ of hash browns in bottom. Top with ⅓ onions, ⅓ ham, and ⅓ cheese. Repeat two more times.

2.	In large mixing bowl, beat together eggs, milk, salt, and pepper until well blended. Pour over ham and potato layers.

3.	Place insert in Instant Pot. Press "Slow Cooker", then "Adjust" until the light comes on under "less", adjust time using plus and minus sign to get it to 7 hours. If you'd like to cook it faster, press "Slow Cooker", don't adjust to less, then adjust time to 3-4 hours.

Boiled Eggs

INGREDIENTS

Pasture raised eggs (see how easy it is already?)

1cup water

INSTRUCTIONS

1. Plug in your Instant Pot
2. Pour one cup water in the bottom of the stainless bowl
3. Place in a stainless strainer/steamer basket
4. Place your desired number of eggs on top of the opened steamer basket
5. Put the lid on
6. Power on and press the MANUAL button
7. With the "-" button adjust it to 8 minutes on the display
8. Close and lock the lid and make sure the vent on top is closed
9. Let the IP do it's magic and then do the quick release valve
10. Let cool slightly and vent completely before opening lid
11. Transfer eggs to fridge or allow to cool slightly before eating right away

Oatmeal

INGREDIENTS

1/2 cup Steel Cut Oats

2 cups water

1 tablespoon oil

Dash of salt

INSTRUCTIONS

1. Combine ingredients in instant pot, select high pressure and set 10 minutes cook time.

2. When beep sounds, turn off instant pot and use a natural pressure release for 10 minutes. Then do a quick pressure release to release any remaining pressure.

3. Top with milk, fresh or dried fruit, chopped nuts or granola, and your favorite sweetener—brown or white sugar, maple syrup, or agave syrup. This time I chose dried blueberries, strawberries, granola and brown sugar.

CHICKEN RECIPES

Coconut Chicken Curry

INGREDIENTS

1 cup full fat coconut milk

¼ c. lemon juice

1 Tbs. curry powder

1 tsp. turmeric

½ tsp. salt

4 lbs. chicken meat of your choice

Optional: ½-1 tsp. lemon zest

INSTRUCTIONS

1. Mix the coconut milk, lemon juice and spices together in a bowl or glass measuring cup. (Don't worry about incorporating that large chunk of coconut cream from the top of the can of coconut milk; just mix the liquidy part together.)

2. Pour a little bit on the bottom of the Instant Pot.

3. Add the chicken.

4. Pour in the rest, including the coconut cream chunk if you've got one, on top of the chicken.

5. Lock in the lid and close the valve.

6. Turn the IP to "poultry" which should be 15 minutes at high pressure.

7. It will take about 20 minutes to get to pressure.

8. After the 15 minute cook time, use the quick release by opening the valve.

9. Test chicken for doneness by cutting open and observing the center (if you see any pink, turn the IP back on for another 5-10 minutes on manual high pressure).

10. Use 2 forks to shred the chicken up in the pot (or remove to a plate if you're having trouble getting it all in the pot).

11. Optional: Add ½-1 tsp. lemon zest after cooking.

12. Serve with steamed or roasted veggies or over rice.

Chicken Tikka Masala

INGREDIENTS

1 to 1 1/2 pounds boneless, skinless chicken thighs

1 large onion, diced

3 cloves garlic, minced

1-inch piece whole ginger, peeled and grated

2 tablespoons tomato paste

1 to 2 tablespoons garam masala

2 teaspoons paprika

2 teaspoons kosher salt

1 (28-ounce) can diced tomatoes

3/4 cup heavy cream or coconut milk

Fresh cilantro, chopped

2 cups cooked rice, to serve

INSTRUCTIONS

1. Cut the chicken meat into bite-sized pieces and transfer them to an instant pot. Stir in the onion, garlic, ginger, tomato paste, 1 tablespoon of garam masala, paprika, and kosher salt until the chicken is evenly covered with spices. Stir in the diced tomatoes with their juices.

   Tip: *If you have the time: Marinate the chicken in 1/2 cup yogurt for up to 6 hours. Shake to remove excess yogurt before transferring to the slow cooker.*

   Tip: *If you have the time: Sauté the onions and garlic in a little olive oil over medium-high heat in a skillet until softened, then stir in the ginger, tomato paste, and spices until fragrant. Transfer to the slow cooker with the chicken and diced tomatoes. This will give your tikka masala more depth of flavor.*

2. Cover the instant pot and set on slow cooker for 4 hours on high or 8 hours on low. Fifteen minutes before the end of cooking, stir in the heavy cream. If you prefer a thicker sauce, leave the slow cooker uncovered for the last 15 minutes. Taste and add more garam masala or salt to taste.

3. Serve over rice with fresh cilantro sprinkled over the top of each serving. The tikka masala can be refrigerated for 3 to 4 days or frozen for 3 to 4 months.

Mexican Chicken Wraps

INGREDIENTS

1-2 T olive oil

1 large onion sliced

1 clove garlic crushed (or 1 tsp garlic powder)

1 Kg of boneless/skinless chicken thighs

1 can green chiles (127 ml)

1 handful fresh cilantro or 1 tsp ground coriander

400 gms of tomatillos or salsa verde

Salt and Pepper

200 gms Garbanzo beans

400 gms leftover rice

400 gms cheddar cheese

200 ml chopped tomatoes

100 ml black olives

INSTRUCTIONS

1. Sauté onions until translucent in oil in the instant pot.
2. When onions are translucent, sauté garlic for 15 seconds. Add chicken, chiles, cilantro (or coriander), tomatillos (or salsa verde), salt and pepper to taste.
3. Pressure cook on "Poultry" for 8 minutes, leave on keep warm for 3 minutes.
4. Release pressure. Remove chicken and break it up with forks.
5. Add garbanzo beans and rice, sautéing for 1 minute.
6. Return meat to reheat and stir in cheese.
7. Serve as meat course, with refried beans salad, and tortillas. Also can be used as a burrito filling. Garnish at the table with chopped tomatoes and black olives.

Spicy Shredded chicken

INGREDIENTS

2 lbs boneless, skinless chicken breasts

2 medium (or large) sized limes

1 1/2 teaspoons chili powder

1 teaspoon cumin

1 teaspoon onion powder

1 teaspoon kosher salt (use a little less is substituting table salt)

1/4 teaspoon black pepper

6 cloves garlic, finely minced or pressed

1/2 teaspoon liquid smoke

INSTRUCTIONS

1. If chicken breasts are more than 1-inch thick, cut in half. Place chicken in pressure cooker pot. Squeeze in the juice of both limes. Sprinkle all seasonings and liquid smoke over chicken and add garlic. Use clean hands to rub spice mixture all over all sides of chicken.

2. Secure lid on pot and cook at high pressure for 6 minutes. When finished let rest for 5 minutes and then release steam. Check temperature of chicken with an instant-read thermometer and make sure internal temperature is at least 165 degrees.

3. Shred chicken and return to pot and toss in juices. Season with additional salt and pepper to taste, if desired.

Chicken Burritos

INGREDIENTS

1 tablespoon olive oil

1 whole boneless skinless chicken breast (about 1 lb or 450g of meat)

1 medium red onion, chopped

1 medium yellow or green bell pepper, chopped

1 cup (200g) dried black beans, soaked overnight

1½ cup (375ml) water

1½ teaspoons salt

1 teaspoon cumin powder

1 teaspoon cayenne pepper

1 teaspoon marjoram

1 teaspoon garlic powder

1 bay leaf

2 cups shredded lettuce or cabbage

For the Rice:

1½ cups (285g) parboiled rice

1½ cups (375ml) water

1 lime zested and juiced (about 1 tablespoon zest and 1 tablespoon juice)

INSTRUCTIONS

1. In a 4-cup (1L) capacity heat-proof bowl, add the parboiled rice, lime zest and water. If the container does not have a handle, make a foil sling. Set the container and sling aside.

2. Add olive oil and brown the chicken on one side (about 5 minutes) in the instant pot. Remove the chicken and add the onion, bell pepper, black beans, herbs and spices, salt, bay leaf and water. Mix well.

3. Lay the chicken breast browned-side up on top of the bean and veggie mixture. Lay the steamer basket or trivet on top of the chicken breast. Rest the heat-proof bowl with the rice mixture on top of the steamer basket. Close and lock the lid of the instant pot. Cook for 6 minutes at high pressure.

4. When done, open the pressure cooker with the Natural release method.

5. Remove the bowl with the rice out of the pressure cooker and set aside. Then, sprinkle lime juice over the rice and fluff with a fork. Remove the trivet or steamer basket and put them to wash. Remove the chicken breast to a plate and with a fork, or two, tease the meat apart. Slide the meat back in the pressure cooker and mix well with the beans.

Cherry Tomato Chicken

INGREDIENTS

1 teaspoon olive oil

3 pounds (1.5 kilos) bone-in chicken legs and thighs

1 pound (500g) cherry tomatoes

2 garlic cloves, crushed.

¼ teaspoon hot pepper flakes (or one fresh hot pepper, chopped)

1 teaspoon salt (use 2 teaspoons if your chicken has not been previously salt-brined)

1 teaspoon dried oregano

¼ cup (60ml) tart red table wine (such as Merlot)

1 cup water

1 sprig fresh basil leaves, torn

½ cup (70g) pitted green olives, rinsed

INSTRUCTIONS

1. In the heated instant pot, add the olive oil and brown the chicken thighs on all sides.

2. Remove the stems from the cherry tomatoes and put them in a large ziploc bag so they are in a single layer. Close the bag almost completely - leave a tiny hole at the end. Or loosely knot a common plastic bag. With a meat pounder, or heavy pot, lightly crush all of the cherry tomatoes - the goal is to burst them open, not flatten them.

3. Set the chicken aside and pour the crushed cherry tomato mixture and all of its juice into the instant pot base. Add the garlic, hot pepper, salt , oregano, wine and water and mix well, scraping up the brown bits of chicken stuck to the bottom of the cooker.

4. Place the chicken back into the instant pot and mix to coat the chicken with the contents of the cooker. Cook for 13-14 minutes at high pressure.

5. When done, open the cooker by releasing the pressure through the valve. Stir the contents and let the cooker stand uncovered for about 5 minutes, stirring occasionally to reduce some of the cooking liquid.

Coconut Chicken

INGREDIENTS

One small chicken – about 4 pounds

1 tablespoon coconut oil

Salt

Pepper

INSTRUCTIONS

1. Turn on the sauté setting and add in the coconut oil. When the oil heats up, place the chicken in breast-down and brown. I move mine around a few times to brown the sides as well.

2. When the chicken is nice and brown, turn it over and sprinkle with seasoning.

3. Lock the lid into place and set the valve to "sealing." Select "Poultry" and then increase the type of pressure from normal to high. (If you have the 7-in-1, you can do that by pressing the "Adjust" button.) Set the time to 20 minutes.

4. When the 20 minutes is up, turn the valve to "venting" and allow to depressurize. Turn the chicken over and then cook for another 15 minutes on high. It should be ready at this point, but check and make sure. If needed, cook for 5 more minutes, then serve.

Honey BBQ Wings

INGREDIENTS

1 cup of your favorite bbq sauce

1/2 cup brown sugar

2 tbs Worcestershire sauce

1 tbs fresh minced garlic

1/2 cup water

1/2 cup of honey

2 lbs chicken wings (frozen or thawed)

Optional: 1/2 teaspoon crushed cayenne pepper to add some heat

INSTRUCTIONS

1. Add all the ingredients to the Instant Pot Electric pressure cooker. Set the valve on top to seal.

2. Frozen chicken wings: set pressure on high for 12 minutes or thawed chicken wings: set pressure on high for 10 minutes

3. Quick release the value on top until all the pressure has released. Carefully remove the lid and place the cooked chicken wings on a pan lined with foil.

4. Baste them with some more bbq sauce.

5. Broil them in the oven on high for 5 minutes to allow the bbq to caramelize.

6. Turn the wings over, baste and then broil for another 2 minutes.

Indian Chicken Curry

INGREDIENTS

1 ½ pounds skinless chicken thighs, cut into bite-sized pieces

2 tablespoons ghee, grassfed butter or fat of choice

1 onion, diced

5 garlic cloves, minced

1-inch knob ginger, minced

1 teaspoon garam masala

1 teaspoon paprika

1 teaspoon coriander powder

1 teaspoon turmeric

1 teaspoon salt

¼ teaspoon cayenne

¼ teaspoon cumin

¼ teaspoon black pepper

1 green bell pepper, chopped in large pieces

1 (15 ounce) can tomato sauce

Add later:

1 cup coconut cream

Pinch of dried fenugreek leaves (kasoori methi)

Cilantro for garnish, optional

INSTRUCTIONS

1. Press the "saute" button on the Instant Pot, and add the ghee and onions to the pot. Stir-fry the onions for 8-10 minutes or until the onions begin to brown.

2. Add the garlic and ginger, stir-fry for 30 seconds.

3. Stir in the spices, then add the chicken and mix until well combined. Continue to stir this for 4-5 minutes to sear the chicken.

4. Add the tomato sauce and green bell pepper, then cover and lock the lid. press the "Keep Warm/Cancel" button on the Instant Pot, then press the "Poultry" button to begin the pressure cooking. It will automatically be set for 15 minutes. Make sure the steam valve is closed.

5. Once the curry is done, the Instant Pot will automatically switch to the "Keep Warm" mode. Allow the pressure to release naturally or use the quick release if you want your food on your plate sooner.

6. Unlock the lid, stir in the coconut cream and fenugreek leaves.

7. Garnish with cilantro if desired, then serve.

Italian Chicken

INGREDIENTS

1 25-oz jar marinara or pasta sauce (where to buy organic pasta sauce)

4 boneless, skinless chicken breasts

1 8-oz package of whole mushrooms, rinsed

INSTRUCTIONS

1. Place chicken breasts in a single layer in the bottom of your Instant Pot (where to buy Instant Pot).
2. Rinse mushrooms and drop on top of the chicken breasts. If using extra veggies, add them with the mushrooms.
3. Pour sauce over chicken and mushrooms then close and lock the lid (I always double check to make sure the sealing ring is in place in the lid!) and make sure the vent is set to SEALING (closed).
4. Press the "Poultry" button. The display should read 15. Allow about 30 mins total cooking time. I prefer to allow the cooker to depressurize naturally but you can use the quick de-pressure method, if desired.
5. Carefully shred the breasts with two forks and mix evenly with the sauce. Serve with your starchy/noodly (where to buy gluten-free pasta) side of choice and enjoy!

Mexican Chicken Chilli

INGREDIENTS

2 lbs Boneless Skinless Chicken Breasts

1 Tbsp Olive Oil

1/2 C. Mild Salsa

1-2 cans of Green Chiles

4 Tbsp Brown Sugar

14.5 oz can Diced Tomatoes

1 Tbsp Chili Powder

1 Tsp Cumin

1 tsp Garlic

1/2 tsp Smoked Paprika

1/2 tsp Oregano

1 1/2 tsp Salt

1/2 tsp Black Pepper

1 tsp Liquid Smoke

INSTRUCTIONS

1. In your empty instant pot, lay the chicken on the bottom and brush with the olive oil.
2. Add all the other ingredients on top of the chicken.
3. Put the lid on the Instant Pot, and close the valve.
4. Set the timer for high (manual) for 27 minutes.
5. When the pot beeps, release the pressure, and remove the chicken to shred. Put the chicken back in and let cook on slow cooker with the lid on for 10-15 more minutes to absorb all the liquid.
6. Serve with hot sauce.

BEEF RECIPES

Corned Beef

INGREDIENTS

3lbs corned beef brisket

20 small red potatoes, whole

1 medium onion, quartered

8 cloves of garlic

4 cups of beef broth

1 head of cabbage

spice packet (often comes with corned beef purchase)

1 bay leaf, crushed

3 whole cloves

20+ peppercorns

20+ coriander

¼ teaspoon allspice

For Gravy:

2 tablespoons cornstarch

INSTRUCTIONS

1.   Place corned beef in the pressure cooker. Add onion, potatoes, and garlic. Pour broth over the meat and veggies. Sprinkle spices over it all. Place lid on instant pot

2.   Cook over high heat until it reaches high pressure. Lower flame and stabilize pressure. Cook for 40 minutes.

3.   Remove from flame and run under cold water to release pressure.

4.   Add cabbage to the pressure cooker. Cook over high flame until it reaches high pressure.

5.   As soon as it reaches high pressure, remove from flame and run under cool water to release pressure.

GRAVY INSTRUCTIONS

1. Remove meat and vegetables from the pressure cooker, but leave the drippings.

2. Add 2 tablespoons of cornstarch to the drippings.

3. Use a whisk to blend the cornstarch into the beef.

4. Cook over a medium flame until it reaches a boil.

5. Lower flame and boil until it thickens, approximately 2 - 3 minutes.

Soy Sauce Beef with Broccoli

INGREDIENTS

1 small onion

3 cloves garlic

1.5 pounds thinly sliced steak

3 tbs sesame oil

3 tbs olive oil

1/3 cup soy sauce

3/4 cup beef broth

1/3 cup brown sugar

Fresh or frozen Broccoli

1 tbs cornstarch

INSTRUCTIONS

1. Place oil and meat on saute in your pot. Saute until meat is brown.
2. Add in onions and garlic and continue to saute until onions are tender.
3. Add in beef broth and soy sauce. Stir in brown sugar and stir until dissolved.
4. Place on 10 minutes high pressure and do a natural release.
5. Mix 2 tbs water with 1 tbs cornstarch and add to your mixture.
6. Mean while steam your broccoli and cook your rice according to directions.
7. Stir in the broccoli and serve over rice.

Beef Taco Meat

INGREDIENTS

2lbs ground beef

1 cup fire roasted salsa

1 teaspoon cumin

1 teaspoon garlic powder

1 teaspoon chili powder

1 teaspoon paprika

1 teaspoon onion powder

1 teaspoon sea salt (or more to taste)

1 teaspoon ground black pepper

1 large yellow onion, diced

1 pastured egg

1/4 cup tapioca starch

1 tablespoon olive oil

INSTRUCTIONS

1. Combine all ingredients in a bowl except for the oil, mixing together well by hand (reserving 1/4 cup of the salsa)

2. Form a loaf with your meat mixture, pressing it together firmly – it can sometimes split while cooking in the Instant Pot (you can also wrap it tightly in foil instead. If you do this, omit the oil and place the foil wrapped meatloaf on the steamer rack and pour in a cup of water underneath)

3. Take your 1 tablespoon of cooking fat and drop it into the stainless bowl of your Instant Pot

4. Now press the "Saute" feature to heat and/or melt the cooking fat

5. Now gently transfer your uncooked meatloaf into the Instant Pot, placing it on the cooking fat

6. Spoon the 1/4 cup of remaining fire roasted salsa on top of your meatloaf

7. Close the lid and select the "Meat/Stew" setting; make sure your display reads "35" minutes and is set on "Normal" pressure

8. Ensure the pressure valve is closed and wait until the cook time has completed before quick releasing the pressure valve

9. Open the lid when safe to do so and carefully remove your meatloaf

10. Serve with fresh cilantro sprigs.

Maple Smoked Beef Brisket

INGREDIENTS

1.5 lb. beef brisket

2 tbsp. maple sugar,

2 tsp. smoked sea salt

1 tsp. black pepper

1 tsp. mustard powder

1 tsp. onion powder

½ tsp. smoked paprika

2 c. bone broth or stock of choice

3 fresh thyme sprigs

INSTRUCTIONS

1. Remove the brisket from the refrigerator about 30 minutes before cooking. Pat it dry with paper towels and set it aside.
2. Mix the spice blend by combining the maple sugar, smoked sea salt, pepper, mustard powder, onion powder, and smoked paprika. Coat the meat generously on all sides. The rub will get a bit sticky due to the sugar.
3. Set your Instant Pot to "Sauté" and allow it to heat up for 2-3 minutes. Grease the bottom with a bit of high heat cooking oil and add the brisket. Brown on all sides until deeply golden but not burnt. Turn the brisket to fatty side up and add the broth, liquid smoke, and thyme to the Instant Pot. Scrape the browned bits off the bottom and cover with the lid.

4. Switch the setting to "Manual" and increase the cook time to 50 minutes. Once finished, allow the Instant Pot to release steam on it's own.

5. Remove the brisket from the pot and cover it with foil to rest. Switch the Instant Pot to "Saute" again to reduce & thicken the sauce (optional) with the lid off for about 10 minutes.

Beef Stew

INGREDIENTS

3 lbs stew beef

1/2 tsp salt

1/2 tsp black pepper

2 tbsp white rice flour (optional)

2 tbsp ghee

1/2 onion, diced

2 cloves garlic, minced

2 tbsp tomato paste

3/4 cup red wine (Zinfandel, Merlot, Cabernet Sauvignon)

3 cups beef broth

3 carrots, peeled and cut into chunks

3 parsnips, peeled and cut into chunks

3 celery stalks, cut into chunks

1.5 lbs waxy potatoes (red, golden, etc), cut into chunks

3 sprigs fresh thyme (1/2 tsp dried okay)

salt and pepper to taste

1 small handful parsley, chopped

INSTRUCTIONS

1. Combine the beef, salt, pepper, and rice flour; toss to dust the beef evenly.

2. Plug in your Instant Pot and press the "Sauté" button. Add the ghee and warm until melted and shimmering, about 3 minutes. Add 1/3 of the beef and sauté until browned, about 6 minutes, then remove the beef and add another 1/3 of the beef. Continue until the rest of the beef has cooked, about 20 minutes total; set the beef aside.

3. Add the onion and sauté until softened, about 4 minutes, then add the garlic and tomato paste. Sauté until aromatic, about 30 seconds, then add the wine and broth. Bring to a simmer, scraping up any browned bits from the bottom of the pot. Add the beef (and any accumulated juices), carrots, parsnips, celery, potatoes, and thyme.

4. Cover and set the Instant Pot to "Meat/Stew" (high pressure) for 20 minutes. Once the Instant Pot finishes, wait until it depressurizes, about 15 minutes. You'll know it's ready when you can remove the lid easily.

5. Gently remove the solid ingredients from the pot (the carrots and parsnips will be very tender) and set aside. Set the Instant Pot to "Sauté" again and simmer the sauce until reduced by half, about 10 minutes. Taste and add salt or pepper if needed. Return the solid ingredients to the pot, stir in the chopped parsley, then serve.

Chunky Beef Curry

INGREDIENTS

1 lb. beef stew meat in chunks

2 tbsp ghee or coconut oil

1 onion

3 large potatoes (or sweet potatoes)

6 carrots

5 cloves garlic

1 cup full fat canned coconut milk

½ cup bone broth or veggie broth

1½ tbsp curry powder

1 tsp sea salt

½ tsp pepper

1 tsp oregano

¼ tsp paprika

INSTRUCTIONS

1. Cut the onion, potatoes and carrots in large chunks. Dice the garlic.
2. Press the saute button on the instant pot and put the ghee in the instant pot. Once the ghee is melted, add the onions and garlic and stir for about 2 minutes.
3. Then, add the stew meat to brown all sides for about 5 minutes.
4. Turn off the instant pot and add the remaining ingredients including the carrots, potatoes, coconut milk, broth, herbs and spices. Stir to make sure all the spices are mixed in the liquid.

5. Place the lid in the locked position and make sure the vent is turned to "sealed". Press the "meat/stew" button and use the +/- buttons to set to 30 minutes. Once you get to 30 minutes it will automatically start cooking.

6. When it's done, serve over cauliflower rice or white rice.

French Beef Stew

INGREDIENTS

6 pieces bacon, chopped

1 large onion, chopped

2 large carrots, peeled and chopped

5 cloves garlic, minced

2 tablespoons tomato paste (I like this one because it comes in a glass jar)

3 lbs. beef stew meat or chuck roast, cut into 2 inch cubes (I used TX Bar Organics)

salt and pepper

1/4 bunch fresh thyme sprigs

1.5 cups Pinot Noir

1.5 cups beef broth

2 bay leaves

2 tablespoons tapioca start (optional for thickening liquid) (I use this one)

1/4 cup fresh parsley leaves, minced for garnish

INSTRUCTIONS

1. Cook bacon until crisp, in a large skillet over medium-high heat. Remove the bacon from the pan with a slotted spoon and set aside. Pour bacon fat into a small bowl or a glass jar, leave enough behind to saute the vegetables, about 1 tablespoon.

2. Add onions and carrots to the skillet and saute until soft, about 5 to 7 minutes, add garlic cloves and tomato paste and saute until tomato paste goes from a bright red to a brick color, about 45 seconds. Transfer the vegetables to the instant pot.

3. Add another tablespoon of bacon fat to the skillet if needed. Generously salt and pepper the beef. Brown the beef in batches,

turning to make sure all sides are browned, about 7 minutes. Transfer browned beef to the instant pot.

4. Add wine, broth, bay leaves, thyme and tapioca starch to the instant pot.

5. Cook on "slow cooker" low for 8 to 10 hours.

6. Discard stems from thyme sprigs and bay leaves.

7. Adjust salt and pepper, garnish with chopped parsley and cooked bacon. Serve and Enjoy!

Tangy Orange Beef

INGREDIENTS

4 pounds bottom roast, cut into cubes

salt and pepper

2 tablespoons olive oil

1 cup beef broth

½ cup soy sauce

5 cloves garlic, minced

1 tablespoon fresh grated ginger

1 pear or Granny Smith apple peeled and chopped

juice of one large orange

INSTRUCTIONS

1. Season the cubed roast liberally with salt and pepper.

2. Heat Instant Pot to saute. Once the pan is hot coat the pan with the olive oil and in batches brown the meat on all the sides. Transfer meat to a plate while you're working.

3. Once all the meat is browned de-glaze the pan with the beef broth, scraping up all the browned bits.

4. Pour in the soy sauce and stir to combine.

5. Return all the meat back to the pan and then place the garlic, ginger and pear on top of the meat, stirring lightly to slightly combine.

6. Finally add in the orange juice.

7. Place the lid on your Instant Pot and using the manual button on normal pressure set to 45 minutes. Make sure the valve is closed.

8. Once the pot is done, release the steam and shred meat using a fork.

9. Serve over rice

Slow Cooked Beef Brisket

INGREDIENTS

3lbs beef brisket

1 large yellow onion

28 ounces canned diced tomatoes with the liquid

1 cup beef stock (chicken stock will work too)

1 head garlic, minced

2 tablespoons olive oil

salt and pepper, to taste

INSTRUCTIONS

1. Rinse beef brisket and pat dry.
2. Grind both salt and pepper over both sides of the meat.
3. Heat a skillet over medium high heat and add one tablespoon of olive oil.
4. Once the oil is hot, sear the brisket on both sides until golden brown, about two minutes per side.
5. In a separate pan, heat over medium heat and add remaining tablespoon of olive oil.
6. Saute onions until golden brown.
7. Add brisket, fatty side down into your slow cooker or Instant Pot.
8. On top of the brisket, place the cooked onion, minced garlic, tomatoes, stock and add a bit more salt and pepper.
9. Cook on the slow cook setting in your Instant Pot for 6 hours.

10. Cooking the meat for 6 hours will allow you to slice it for a nice presentation. If you like your meat more tender so that it falls apart, cook for 8 hours total .

Sloppy Joes

INGREDIENTS

2 lbs ground beef

1 cup ketchup

14 oz can, stewed tomatoes

1/2 cup chopped peppers and onions

2 teaspoon granulated garlic

1 teaspoon onion powder

1 tablespoon Worcestershire

2 tablespoons brown sugar

2 tablespoons chile powder

1 teaspoon dried mustard (or yellow mustard)

Hot sauce to taste

INSTRUCTIONS

1. On Saute, (highest setting) brown ground beef.
2. Stir the rest of the ingredients together in a bowl. Pour over the beef and stir well.
3. Close the lid and set the valve to sealing. Set the pressure to high and time for 8 minutes.
4. If you do not own a pressure cooker, you can cook this recipe on the stove. You will just brown the beef in a pan and then simmer in the sauce stirring occasionally for 20-30 minutes.
5. Serve on your favorite roll. In the photo I used dinner rolls to make sloppy joe sliders.

PORK RECIPES

Kalua Pork

INGREDIENTS

3 slices of bacon

5lbs bone-in pork shoulder roast

5 peeled garlic cloves (optional)

1½ tablespoons Coarse Sea Salt

1 cup water

1 cabbage, cored, and cut into 6 wedges

INSTRUCTIONS

1. Drape three pieces of bacon on the bottom of your Instant Pot. Press the "Sauté " button and in about a minute, your bacon will start sizzling.

2. Slice it into three equal pieces. I normally cut out the piece with the bone first, and then cut the two other pieces to match the first.

3. If you've got some garlic on hand, use it! With a sharp paring knife, stab a few slits in each piece of pork, and tuck in the garlic cloves.

4. Use ¾ teaspoon of medium-coarse salt for every 1 pound of meat and liberally salt your meat.

5. As you're seasoning the pork, you'll hear the bacon sputtering in the pressure cooker. Don't forget to flip the slices, and turn off the heat when the bacon is browned on both sides.

6. Place the salted pork on top of the bacon, keeping the meat in a single layer.

7. Pour in the water.

8. Check your manual to see what the minimum amount of liquid is for your particular model, and adjust accordingly.

9. Cover and lock the lid. If you're using an Instant Pot, select the "Manual" button and press the "+" button until you hit 90 minutes under high pressure. Once the pot is programmed, walk away.

Pulled Pork

INGREDIENTS

3lbs pork butt or pork shoulder

Kosher salt and freshly-ground black pepper

2lbs small red potatoes, scrubbed and cut into sixths

1 tablespoon vegetable oil

1 4oz can Thai green curry paste, such as Maesri

1 15oz can coconut milk

Chopped cilantro or chives, to serve (optional)

Toasted unsweetened coconut, to serve (optional)

INSTRUCTIONS

1. Heat the broiler. Cut the pork into four pieces and sprinkle liberally with salt and pepper. Place on a large baking sheet and broil, turning once, for 15 to 20 minutes or until well-browned.

2. Spread the cut potatoes in the instant pot. Sprinkle them lightly with salt and pepper.

3. While the pork is browning in the oven, fry the curry paste. In a large skillet heat the vegetable oil over medium-high heat. When it is hot, add the curry paste and fry for about 3 to 5 minutes or until the paste smells aromatic and has begun to absorb the oil. Whisk in the coconut milk and cook for another few minutes, or until the coconut milk begins to bubble.

4. Take the browned pork out of the oven and drain away any liquid fat. Arrange the pork in the slow cooker with the potatoes, and pour the hot green curry and coconut milk mixture over it.

5. Cook for 6 to 8 hours on LOW. At the end of cooking shred the pork with two forks; it should be meltingly-tender. (Depending on how

much fat is released from the pork, the curry sauce will not look thick and creamy; it will probably be thin.)

6. Taste and season if necessary with salt or soy sauce. Serve with brown rice, and small bowls of chopped cilantro or chives and toasted unsweetened coconut.

Asian Pork Ribs

INGREDIENTS

1 Tb oil

1 medium onion sliced

1/4 cup ketchup

1/4 soy sauce

1/3 cup brown sugar

1/3 cup rice wine (or cider) vinegar

1 20 oz can of pineapple

2 cloves garlic chopped

1 tsp. finely chopped ginger

1 tsp. fish sauce (optional)

1 tsp. chili powder

1 tsp. ground coriander

Pinch of smoked paprika

Salt and pepper to taste

4 lbs of ribs, trimmed and cut for serving.

Corn starch

INSTRUCTIONS

1. Directions are for Instant Pot 6-in-1 Pressure Cooker.
2. Add oil, sauté onions until just translucent.
3. Add the rest of the ingredients except cornstarch. Make sure spareribs are submerged in sauce. You can marinate refrigerated in the pot for several hours.

4. Pressure cook on "Stew" for 12 minutes, leave on keep warm for 3 minutes. Release pressure. Check meat for doneness and moisture. If needs more time set timer to "Stew" for a few more minutes.

5. When meat is done, remove meat to bowl and adjust seasoning (if needed). Set to sauté, when sauce starts to boil, mix cornstarch and water to thicken sauce; taste and stir for one minute.

6. Serve with rice and veggies of your choice.

7. Variation, brown meat in oil on sauté before cooking. Alternately, "char" firmer meat on bbq or under broiler after pressure cooking, basting with strained sauce. Either of these are preferable if you aren't using fish sauce.

BBQ Ribs

INGREDIENTS

2 racks of pork ribs

3 c. Sweet Baby Ray's original BBQ sauce

1 c. of water

2 yellow onions, diced

2 tbs. heaping minced garlic

1 tsp. liquid smoke

1 tbs. chili powder

INSTRUCTIONS

1. Cut ribs into 3 rib portions and place them into Instant Pot Programmable Pressure Cooker. If frozen, no need to defrost. Add all ingredients in a bowl with the BBQ sauce and mix well, then add to the pot. Close the lid. Then press Meat button and set + to 40mins.
2. Once it is done, use the quick pressure release. Open the lid and ensure the ribs are soaked in the sauce, tender and the meat is still on the bone. If not done, use the manual setting and cook for 5 more mins.
3. Remove the meat, cut ribs into individual pieces and put into a large pan with an aluminum foil cover in the oven at 210 degrees. Use the manual setting but reduce the pressure/temp. to "normal". You want to reduce the BBQ sauce by about a cup....i.e., thicken the sauce. Once thickened, serve the hot ribs with the sauce.

Adobo Pork

INGREDIENTS

2 ½ lbs trimmed, boneless pork shoulder blade roast

2 teaspoons kosher salt

black pepper, to taste

6 cloves garlic, cut into sliver

1 1/2 teaspoons cumin

1/2 teaspoon sazon

1/4 teaspoon dry oregano

3/4 cup reduced sodium chicken broth

2-3 chipotle peppers in adobo sauce (to taste)

2 bay leaves

1/4 teaspoon dry adobo seasoning

1/2 teaspoon garlic powder

INSTRUCTIONS

1. Season pork with salt and pepper. In a large skillet brown pork on all sides on high heat for about 5 minutes. Remove from heat and allow to cool.

2. Using a sharp knife, insert blade into pork about 1-inch deep, and insert the garlic slivers, you'll want to do this all over. Season pork with cumin, sazon, oregano, adobo and garlic powder all over.

3. Pour chicken broth in the instant pot, add chipotle peppers and stir, add bay leaves and place pork in the Instant Pot, cover and cook using

the pressure cooker setting on high pressure with the meat button for 50 minutes.

4. When the pressure releases, shred pork using two forks and combine well with the juices that accumalated at the bottom. Remove bay leaves and adjust cumin and add adobo and mix well.

Roast Pork

INGREDIENTS

3lbs pork roast preferably a fatty cut

1teaspoon sea salt (real salt)

1/2teaspoon black pepper

4cups chopped cauliflower

1medium onion, chopped

4cloves garlic

2ribs celery

8ounces portabella mushrooms sliced

2tablespoons organic coconut oil or ghee

2cups filtered water

INSTRUCTIONS

1. In the bottom of your instant pot, place cauliflower, onion, garlic, celery and water. Top with pork roast and season with sea salt & pepper.
2. Cook under pressure for 90 minutes if your roast is frozen, 60 minutes if completely thawed. Quick depressurize following manufactures directions.
3. Carefully remove pork roast from the pressure cooker and place in an oven proof dish. Bake at 400 degrees while preparing the gravy, this helps to render the fat and crisp up the edges of the pork to be more like as if it was slow roasted.
4. Transfer cooked vegetables and broth to your blender and blend until smooth, set aside.

5. In your (dirty) instant pot (on the saute function) cook mushrooms in coconut oil until soft, roughly 3-5 minutes. Add blended vegetables and continue to cook on the saute function until it is thickened as desired.

6. Serve mushroom gravy over shredded pork.

Easy Leftover BBQ Pork

INGREDIENTS

3lbs Pork Roast

Any spices you'd like. (salt, pepper, chives, Worcestershire)

1/4 cup of Vegetable oil

2 cups of chicken stock or water

BBQ sauce

INSTRUCTIONS

1. First start by prepping your work station. I cut my roast in half to make it easier to fit and handle. Spice up the roast with whatever you want or marinade and let sit for about 20 minutes if you want.
2. Now Get your pressure cooker and turn on the saute button and let it warm up with the vegetable oil inside it. When it's hot, add your pork. Sear each side of the pork for 3 minutes.
3. Now you want to add 2 cups of liquid (Chicken stock or water).
4. Now close the lid on the pot and hit Meat/Stew button and Add 90 minutes to the time. Make sure your seal is closed. (I forget this sometimes, lol) Now, sit back and wait for it to count down to 1!
5. Once it is done, let is naturally release for 10 minutes.

SEAFOOD RECIPES

Quick n Simple Seafood Pasta

INGREDIENTS

1 tbsp extra virgin olive oil

80 g onion, chopped

2 garlic cloves, chopped

1 small carrot, chopped

1 quarter red pepper, chopped

80 ml dry white wine

130 g frozen mixed seafood, straight from freezer

460 ml vegetable stock

140 g macaroni

1 tbsp tomato purée

1 tsp mixed herbs

Salt

Black pepper, freshly ground

Fresh lime or lemon juice (optional)

INSTRUCTIONS

1. In the Instant Pot, press the Sauté button, add the olive oil and fry the vegetables for 3-5 minutes.

2. Add the wine, stir and let bubble for a minute or two, lid off. Press Keep Warm/Cancel button.

3. Add seafood, stock, macaroni, mixed herbs, tomato purée, a pinch of salt and pepper. Stir.

4. Press Manual button, programme 5 minutes.

5. Do a quick release after letting it rest for 30 seconds and then remove the lid

and let it rest for a couple of minutes, it will be quite liquid to start with but will thicken rather quickly. So finish setting the table, pouring a glass of wine or, if you prefer, clearing up.

Seafood Chowder

INGREDIENTS

2 can minced clams

2 can crabmeat

1 can oysters

1 stick butter

1 medium onion, chopped

1 lb shrimp (16-20)

1 lb scallops

1 S&P to taste

2 cup heavy cream

2 cup half and half

1 your favorite fish, cut up and deboned

INSTRUCTIONS

1.   Melt butter in a 6 qt pan. Saute onions. Then saute the shrimp on medium heat. Add the heavy cream and half and half. Now add the clams, crabmeat, scallops, oysters and S&P. Add any other fish you want in at this time.

2.   Cook this on low for 1-2 hours on "slow cooker".

Crispy Salmon

INGREDIENTS

2 frozen salmon fillets (1 inch in thickness)

1 cup (250 ml) cold running tap water

2 tablespoons olive oil

Kosher salt and Ground black pepper to Taste

INSTRUCTIONS

1. Pour 1 cup of cold running tap water into the instant pot. Place the Frozen Salmon Fillets on top of a steamer rack. Close the lid and cook at Low Pressure for 1 minute. Turn off the heat and do a Quick Release. Open the lid carefully. Remove the salmon fillets and pat them dry with paper towels.

2. Preheat a Skillet: Heat a skillet over medium high heat.

3. Season the Salmon Fillets: Add a tablespoon of olive oil on the salmon skin. Season generously with kosher salt and ground black pepper.

4. Crisp the Salmon Skin: Make sure the skillet is hot to prevent the skin from sticking to the skillet. Place the salmon fillet skin side down for 1 – 2 minutes.

5. Serve: Remove the salmon fillets from the skillet and serve with your favorite side dishes.

Coconut Fish Curry

INGREDIENTS

1lb Fish steaks or fillets, rinsed and cut into bite-size pieces (fresh or frozen)

1 Tomato, chopped

2 Green Chiles, sliced into strips

2 Medium onions, sliced into strips

2 Garlic cloves, squeezed

1 Tbsp. freshly grated Ginger

6 Curry leaves

1 Tbsp. ground Coriander

2 tsp. ground Cumin

½ tsp. ground Turmeric

1 tsp. Chili Powder

½ tsp. Ground Fenugreek (Methi)

2 cups un-sweetened Coconut Milk

Salt to taste

Lemon juice to taste

INSTRUCTIONS

1. In the preheated instant pot on medium-low heat without the lid, add a swirl of oil and then drop in the curry leaves and lightly fry them until golden around the edges (about 1 minute).

2. Then add the onion, garlic and ginger and sautee until the onion is soft. Add all of the ground spices: Coriander, Cumin, Tumeric, Chili

Powder and Fenugreek and sautee them together with the onions until they have released their aroma (about 2 minutes).

3. De-glaze with the coconut milk making sure to un-stick anything from the bottom of the cooker and incorporate it in the sauce. Add the Green Chiles, Tomatoes and fish pieces. Stir to coat the fish well with the mixture. Set the pressure level to LOW. Turn the heat up high and when the pan reaches pressure, lower the heat and count 5 minutes cooking time at LOW pressure (or 2-3 at HIGH).

4. When time is up, release pressure using the Normal method - release vapor through the valve. Add salt to taste and spritz with lemon juice just before serving. Serve alone, or with steamed rice.

Mediterranean Chicken Prawn Rice

INGREDIENTS

2 Tbsp olive oil

1 lb chicken breasts and thighs diced

1 lb prawns

2 cups yellow onions, finely diced

2 cups tri-color bell peppers, dices

2 Tbsp garlic, minced

1 1/2 cups rice

3 1/2 cups chicken stock

1 cup crushed tomatoes

1 Tbsp plus 1 tsp creole seasoning

1 Tbsp Worcestershire sauce

1 lb Andouille sausage, pre-cooked and sliced

INSTRUCTIONS

1. Set Instant Pot to "Saute". Coat chicken with 1 Tbsp creole seasoning, and brown the meat on all sides. Remove the chicken from heat and set aside.

2. Add onions, peppers, and garlic, and sauce until the onions are translucent. Add rice, and sauce for 2 minutes. Add tomato puree, creole seasoning, Worcestershire, and chicken. Close the lid and press "Rice".

3. When the rice is cooked, release steam, remove the lid, and add sausage and prawns. Place lid back on the Instant Pot, press "Manual", and cook an additional 2 minutes.

Shrimp Rice

INGREDIENTS

1lbs frozen wild caught shrimp, shell & tail on

1 cup Jasmine Rice

¼ cup butter

¼ cup chopped fresh Parsley

1 teaspoon sea salt (real salt)

¼ teaspoon black pepper

1 pinch crushed red pepper or to taste

1 medium lemon, juiced

1 pinch saffron

1 ½ cups filtered water or chicken broth

4 cloves garlic minced or pressed

Optional Garnishes

Butter

Grated hard cheese

Chopped fresh Parsley

Fresh Lemon Juice

INSTRUCTIONS

1. Combine all ingredients in your pressure cooker, layering the frozen-shell-on-shrimp on the top.
2. Secure lid and cook under high pressure for 5 minutes.

3. Quickly depressurize by turning the valve

4. The paella can be served with the shells on the shrimp or, If desired, gently remove cooked shrimp from the rice and peel. Add peeled shrimp back into the rice and serve. discard the shells.

5. Serve each serving with a garnish of fresh parsley, butter, grated cheese and squeeze of lemon juice.

VEGETARIAN RECIPES

Indian Savory Oats Hash

INGREDIENTS

1½ cup old-fashioned oats

3 tablespoon raw peanuts

1 teaspoon safflower or other neutral oil

½ teaspoon black mustard seeds

10 curry leaves, chopped

⅛ teaspoon asafetida

1 hot green chili, finely chopped

½ cup finely chopped red onion

½ teaspoon turmeric

¼ teaspoon cayenne / red chili powder or to taste

¾ to 1 teaspoon salt

⅓ cup fresh or frozen green peas, thawed if frozen

¼ teaspoon sugar

2 tablespoons chopped cilantro, for garnish

1 teaspoon lemon juice, for garnish (not optional)

INSTRUCTIONS

1. Wash the oats and soak in 2 cups of water for 7 to 8 minutes. (Steps 2 through 4 take about the same time, so the oats do not have to be soaked in advance.)
2. Heat a skillet over medium heat. Add the peanuts and dry roast until they change color slightly, about 2 minutes. Remove from the skillet and set aside.

3. In the same skillet, heat the oil over medium heat. When the oil is hot, add the mustard seeds and curry leaves. Let the mustard seeds start to pop, 30 seconds. Add the asafetida and chili, then stir in the onions and cook until translucent, 5 to 6 minutes. After the onions are done, you can add other veggies if using and cook then until al-dente.

4. Add the salt, turmeric, cayenne, peas, and sugar and mix well. Cook for 1 minute.

5. Drain the oats well and add to the pan, then stir in the roasted nuts. Mix well. Cover, reduce the heat to medium-low, and cook for 4 to 5 minutes or until the oats are tender, but not mushy like oatmeal. Stir to mix and fluff. Taste and adjust salt and spice. Cover and set aside for 2 minutes. Serve warm, garnished with cilantro and a generous drizzle of lemon juice.

Bean vegetable stew

INGREDIENTS

2 tbsp lard or olive oil

2 stalks celery, diced

1 large onion, diced

1 large carrot, diced

3 cloves garlic, minced

1 tsp dried oregano

1 tsp dried basil

Sea salt and pepper, to taste

28 oz can San Marzano tomatoes

15 oz can (or about 2 cups freshly cooked, drained) white or cannellini beans

4 cups bone broth or vegetable broth

1 bay leaf

1/2 cup fresh spinach or kale (without the rib) torn into shreds

1 cup gluten-free elbow pasta

1/3 cup finely grated parmesan cheese (omit for vegan option)

1-2 tbsp fresh pesto (optional)

INSTRUCTIONS

1. Set Instant Pot to saute mode. Add olive oil, onion, carrot, celery and garlic. Mix until softened.
2. Add basil, oregano, salt and pepper.

3. If canned tomatoes are still whole, pulse tomatoes and liquid in can in a food processor or blender for a few seconds to dice tomatoes.

4. Add tomatoes, bone broth, spinach or kale, bay leaf, and pasta. Close lid and set to manual high pressure (HP) for 6 minutes. It will take about 8 minutes for the Instant Pot to reach high pressure, then it will cook for 6 minutes.

5. When timer goes off, let sit for 1-2 minutes. Then set to quick pressure release to vent steam.

6. Remove lid and add white kidney beans.

7. Serve in bowls and garnish with parmesan cheese and a dollop of pesto.

Refried Beans

INGREDIENTS

2lbs dried pinto beans, sorted

1 1/2 cups chopped onion

4-5 garlic cloves, roughly chopped

1 jalapeno, seeded and chopped

2 teaspoons dried oregano

1 1/2 teaspoons ground cumin

1/2 teaspoon ground black pepper

3 tablespoons lard, or vegetable shortening for vegan

4 cups chicken broth, or vegetable broth for vegan

4 cups water

1-2 teaspoons sea salt

INSTRUCTIONS

1. In a large mixing bowl, add the sorted dried pinto beans and fill the bowl with enough water to cover the beans by several inches. Set aside to soak for 15 minutes while you prepare the remaining ingredients.
2. To the Instant Pot bowl, add the chopped onion, garlic cloves, jalapeno, dried oregano, ground cumin, ground black pepper, lard, chicken broth, and water.
3. Use a colander to strain the beans and discard the soaking liquid. Rinse with fresh water.

4. Now add the beans to the Instant Pot bowl, and stir all of the ingredients together. It's okay if the lard is in a solid lump, as soon as the Instant Pot comes up to pressure/temperature, the lard will melt.

5. Place the lid on the Instant Pot and ensure the steam release valve is set to sealing. Press the "Bean/Chili" key, which will show 30 minutes of cooking time, and increase the time to 45 minutes. Now walk away. When the Instant Pot is done cooking, it will come down from pressure naturally, about 40 minutes.

6. When the pressure is released, open the lid of the Instant Pot and add the sea salt to taste. Use an immersion blender to blend the beans to the desired consistency. The beans will appear soupy, but will thicken as they cool.

Ratatouille

INGREDIENTS

4 tablespoons olive oil, divided, plus more for drizzling

2 medium yellow onions, diced

1lb eggplant

1lb zucchini or summer squash

2 large red, green, or yellow bell peppers (about 1 pound)

1lb tomatoes

4 cloves garlic

2 tablespoons tomato paste

1/2 teaspoon fine salt, plus more for seasoning

1/4 cup coarsely chopped fresh basil leaves

INSTRUCTIONS

1. Heat 2 tablespoons of the oil in a large frying pan over medium heat until shimmering. Add the onions, season with salt, and cook, stirring occasionally and adjusting the heat as needed, until completely softened and light golden-brown, about 30 minutes. Meanwhile, prepare the rest of the vegetables.

2. Trim the eggplant and zucchini, cut into 1-inch cubes, and place in the insert of a 6-quart or larger slow cooker. Trim, core, and cut the bell peppers into 1-inch dice and add to the instant pot. Core the tomatoes, cut into 1 1/2-inch dice, and add to the instant pot. Finely chop the garlic and add to the instant pot.

3. When the onions are ready, add the tomato paste to the pan and stir to coat the onions. Transfer the onion mixture to the instant pot. Add the remaining 2 tablespoons oil and 1/2 teaspoon salt. Stir to coat all the vegetables.

4. Place in the instant pot and turn on slow cooker mode and cook until the vegetables are extremely tender, 4 hours on high or 5 to 6 hours on low. If you'd like to cook off some of the excess liquid in the instant pot, cook uncovered for the last 30 minutes.

5. Stir in the basil and taste for seasoning, adding more salt as needed. Drizzle with more olive oil before serving if desired.

Red Lentils and Sweet Potato

INGREDIENTS

1 small/medium onion, peeled and diced

1 sweet potato, peeled and chopped

1/2 cup red lentils, rinsed

1/2 tsp cinnamon

1/4 tsp chipotle chili pepper powder (mine is Kroger grocery store brand)

1/4 tsp garlic powder

2 tablespoons Sushi Rice Vinegar

1 tablespoon nutritional yeast flakes

1 1/2 cups water

INSTRUCTIONS

1. Place all items in Instant Pot electric pressure cooker. Stir to combine. Cook on high pressure for 5 minutes.
2. Release the pressure.

Indian Kadhi

INGREDIENTS

To put in blender:

1/2 cup gram flour

1 cup yogurt

5-6 cups water

1 tsp salt

1 tsp turmeric

For basic seasoning:

1/2 tsp fenugreek seeds

1 tsp Ajwain seeds

4 dry red chilies

INSTRUCTIONS

1. Use a blender to blend together gram flour, yogurt, water, turmeric and salt.

2. Using "Saute" function in Instant pot, prepare a basic seasoning by heating 1 tsp oil/ghee and adding the fenugreek seeds, ajwain seeds and the red chilies. When the aroma tells you they are ready (in a few seconds to a minute), add the blended mixture in to this.
   You can also prepare basic seasoning in a saute pan and pour in to the yogurt blended mixture.

3. Cook this mixture using the "Slow cook" setting for 4 hours.

Butternut Squash Risotto

INGREDIENTS

A dab of oil for sautéing the vegetables

1/2 a cup of chopped onion

3 cloves of minced garlic

1 red bell pepper, diced

2 cups of peeled and diced butternut squash

1 + 1/2 cups of Arborio (risotto) rice

3 + 1/2 cups of vegetable broth

1/2 a cup dry white wine

1 package of white mushrooms (8 oz)

1 teaspoons salt

1 teaspoon black pepper

1/2 teaspoon coriander

1/4 teaspoon oregano

About 3 cups of greens - I used a spinach, kale and chard mixture

1 large handful of parsley

1 + 1/2 a tablespoon nutritional yeast

INSTRUCTIONS

1. Using the saute feature, heat the Instant Pot with a bit of oil
2. Add the onion, garlic, bell pepper and butternut squash and saute for about 3 - 5 minutes or until starting to brown
3. Add the rice, and stir well.

4. Add the vegetable broth, wine, mushrooms, salt, black pepper, coriander and oregano and stir well.

5. Close the lid and put the pressure valve to "sealed"

6. Click "manual" and reduce the time to 5 minutes

7. When Instant Pot finishes, carefully release the pressure immediately

8. Stir in greens, parsley and nutritional yeast and let sit for about 5 minutes to thicken

Vegan Chili

INGREDIENTS

1lbs of red lentils

7 cups of water, divided

2 14.5 ounce cans salt-free diced tomatoes

1 6oz can salt-free tomato paste

10oz chopped onion

1lb red bell pepper

3oz pitted dates

8 cloves of garlic, finely minced

4 Tablespoons Apple Cider Vinegar

1 1/2 Tbsp parsley flakes

1 1/2 Tbsp oregano

1 1/2 Tbsp salt-free chili powder

2 tsp SMOKED paprika

½ teaspoon chipotle powder

¼ teaspoon crushed red pepper flakes

INSTRUCTIONS

1. Blend the dates, garlic, red bell pepper, tomatoes and one cup of the water in a blender until smooth.
2. Place all remaining ingredients (including date mixture) in an Instant Pot and cook on high for 10 minutes. Let pressure release naturally or release and enjoy immediately.

Vegetable Soup

INGREDIENTS

2 cloves garlic, minced

1/2 onion, diced

2 ribs celery, diced

1 carrot, peeled and diced

1/2 cup frozen corn kernels

4 cups diced potatoes, peeled (about 5-6 medium size)

3 cups vegetable broth

1/2 tsp dried dill

1/2 tsp celery salt

salt/pepper to taste

1 cup chopped kale

1/4 cup coconut milk

Hot sauce to taste

INSTRUCTION

1. Sauté the onion and garlic with 1-2 tbsp water in a soup pot over medium heat for about 3 minutes until starting to soften

2. Add the carrot and celery and sauté 3-4 more minutes. Add another tbsp or 2 of water if needed so the vegetables don't stick.

3. Add the vegetable broth, potatoes, dill, celery salt, salt and pepper.

4. Bring to a boil, reduce heat to low and simmer for 15 minutes until potatoes are tender.

5. Using an immersion blender , puree about 1/4 - 1/3 of the soup to create a

thick creamy base. (alternatively, take about 2 cups of the soup and purée it in a blender and then return it to the soup pot).

6. Add the corn and kale, stir to combine and simmer 5 more minutes to heat through.

7. Take off heat and add coconut milk, if using.

8. Serve with a few dashes of hot sauce if desired.

Rosemary Mashed Potatoes

INGREDIENTS

5-6 Large Potatoes Peeled and cubed

1 cup chicken broth

3 cloves garlic

1 sprig rosemary

2 tbs butter

¼ cup milk

INSTRUCTIONS

1. Place cubed potatoes in the Instant pot with chicken broth whole cloves of garlic, rosemary sprig, and butter.
2. Place instant pot on manual high pressure for 25 minutes. Do a quick release.
3. Drain Potatoes and add milk and butter I put mine in my kitchen aid and mixed it on high for 1 minute.
4. You do not have to use your mixer just simply mash potatoes with your hand held masher for 3-4 minutes or until creamy and smooth. I hope you like these as much as I do.

Cauliflower Rice

INGREDIENTS

1 medium to large head of cauliflower

2 Tbs. olive oil

¼ tsp. salt(more to taste)

½ tsp. dried parsley

optional seasonings to play with:

¼ tsp. cumin (or find on Amazon)

¼ tsp. turmeric (or find on Amazon)

¼ tsp. paprika

fresh cilantro

lime wedges (or lime juice)

INSTRUCTIONS

1. Wash cauliflower and trim off the leaves. Usually this means you'll chop it into a few large pieces.
2. Put all the pieces into the steamer insert in an Instant Pot.
3. Pour one cup water under the cauliflower and steamer basket.
4. Close and lock the lid. Make sure the valve is closed.
5. Set on manual for one minute.
6. After the cook timer beeps, open the valve to quick-release the pressure.
7. Remove the cauliflower to a plate.
8. Pour out the water in the pot.
9. Return the pot to the cooker and press cancel, then the saute button.

10. Add the oil to the pot, then the cooked cauliflower.

11. Break up with a potato masher.

12. Add desired spices while stirring and heating. Salt and parsley makes a pretty basic cauli rice ready for any saucy dish on top.

13. Use the optional spices and serve with fresh cilantro and a squeeze of lime juice for a delicious "cilantro lime" version, or try your own! You can shake a few seasonings in, taste it, and keep trying things.

DESSERT RECIPES

Caramel, Pecan Cheesecake

INGREDIENTS

3/4 cup Ginger Snaps (about 20 cookies)

2 tablespoons pecans

2 tablespoons butter, melted

2 8 ounce packages cream cheese, at room temperature

1/2 cup granulated sugar

1/2 cup pumpkin

1 1/2 teaspoons pumpkin pie spice

1/2 teaspoon vanilla extract

2 large eggs

Topping:

14 caramels

2 tablespoons milk

2 tablespoons chopped pecans

INSTRUCTIONS

1. Prepare a foil sling for lifting the pan out of the instant pot by taking an 18" strip of foil and folding it twice lengthwise. Set aside.
2. In a blender or food processor, combine cookies and pecans. Pulse until finely chopped. In a small bowl, mix cookie crumbs and melted butter until well combined.
3. Use your fingers or the bottom of a drinking glass and press crumbs firmly into the bottom and up the sides of a 7" spring form pan. Put the pan in the freezer until ready to use.

4. In a large mixing bowl, mix the cream cheese and sugar until smooth. Add pumpkin, pumpkin pie spice, and vanilla and mix well. Add in eggs one at a time and mix on low speed just until blended. Do not overwork the batter.

5. Pour batter into the spring form pan on top of the crust.

6. Pour 1 cup of water into the instant pot and place the trivet in the bottom. Carefully center the spring form pan on the foil strip and lower it into the instant pot. Fold the foil strips down so that they do not interfere with closing the lid.

7. Lock the lid in place. Select High Pressure and set the timer for 15 minutes. (25 minutes if you like a denser cheesecake.) When beep sounds, turn off pressure cooker and use a natural pressure release for 10 minutes and then do a quick pressure release to release any remaining pressure. When valve drops carefully remove lid.

8. Remove spring form pan to a wire rack to cool. If there is a little water on top of the cheesecake, gently blot with a paper towel. When cheesecake is completely cooled, refrigerate covered with plastic wrap for at least 4 hours or overnight.

9. To serve: Microwave caramels and milk in microwaveable bowl on high for 1 1/2 minutes or until caramels are completely melted, stirring every 30 seconds. Spoon over individual servings of cheesecake. Sprinkle with chopped pecans.

Stuffed Peaches

INGREDIENTS

5 medium organic peaches or 6 small peaches*

1/4 cup Otto's cassava flour

1/4 cup maple sugar

2 tablespoons grass fed butter

1/2 teaspoon ground cinnamon

1/4 teaspoon pure almond extract

Pinch Celtic sea salt

1/4 teaspoon pure almond extract

INSTRUCTIONS

1. Slice 1/4 inch off the tops of peaches, discard. Using a sharp paring knife, cut around and remove the pits so the peaches are hollowed out. Leave at least 1/2 inch of flesh so the peaches stay intact. If the peaches are very firm, use a spoon to help loosen and scoop out the pit and the flesh around it. Set aside.

2. Prepare the crumble mixture. In a mixing bowl or shallow dish, add cassava flour, unrefined sweetener of choice, butter, cinnamon, almond extract and sea salt. With clean hands, mix the everything together until the mixture is crumbly.

3. Fill and top hollowed peaches with the crumble mixture.

4. Place Instant Pot steamer insert or steamer basket to the Instant Pot. Add water and 1/4 teaspoon almond extract to the Instant Pot. Carefully place stuffed peaches into the Instant Pot on top of the steamer insert.

5. Close and lock the lid of the Instant Pot, making sure the steam release valve is sealed.

6. Turn Instant Pot on by plugging it in, press Manual and decrease time by pressing "-" to 3 minutes. The Instant Pot will say "On" then begin to build pressure and start the countdown.

7. When the Instant Pot is done and beeps, press "Keep Warm/Cancel", unplug, and use an oven mitt to "quick release"/open the steam release valve. When the steam venting stops and the silver dial drops, carefully open the lid.

8. Using an oven mitt and tongs, carefully lift up and remove the steamer insert and place on a dish. Allow stuffed peaches to rest and cool for about 10 minutes. Serve with vanilla ice cream.

Tapioca Pudding

INGREDIENTS

⅓ cup (60g) seed tapioca pearls

1¼ cups (300g) whole milk (or your favorite milk alternative)

½ cup (115g) water

½ cup (100g) sugar

½ lemon, zested

INSTRUCTIONS

1. Prepare the instant pot by adding one cup of water and the steamer basket and set aside.
2. Rinse tapioca pearls in a fine-mesh strainer.
3. To a 4-cup capacity heat-proof bowl add the tapioca pearls, milk, water, lemon zest and sugar. Mix well until the sugar has dissolved and you no longer feel the grit of it at the base. If the container does not have handles to easily lower and lift it from the pressure cooker, construct a foil sling.
4. Lower heat-proof bowl into the instant pot. Cook for 8 minutes at high pressure.
5. When 8 minutes have past, open the pressure cooker with the Natural release method
6. Once the pressure has released let the mixture stand in the closed cooker for an additional 5 minutes before opening

the lid (the milk in the container will boil over if you open the lid too quickly after pressure is released).

7. Carefully lift out the heat-proof bowl and stir vigorously with a fork before distributing into serving bowls, glasses or forms.

8. Cover tightly with cling-wrap and let cool before refrigerating for at least 3 hours, or overnight, before serving or serve warm with the modifications in the notes of this recipe. Serve as-is or topped with seasonal fruit.

Mini Pumpkin Pies

INGREDIENTS

2 lbs butternut squash, peeled and diced

1 cup whole milk (or fresh cream, or coconut milk)

¾ cup 100% pure maple syrup

2 large eggs

1 teaspoon powdered cinnamon

½ teaspoon, powdered ginger (or 1" piece fresh ginger, peeled & very finely chopped)

¼ teaspoon powdered cloves

1 tablespoon organic corn starch

2 pinches sea salt

Garnish: sweetened whipped cream chopped pecans

INSTRUCTIONS

1. Prepare the instant pot by adding 1 cup (250ml) water, or your pressure cooker's minimum liquid requirement, and add the squash cubes to the steamer basket and lower into the pressure cooker. Close and lock the lid of the instant pot. Cook for 3-4 minutes at high pressure (7-9 minutes for pumpkin wedges).

2. In the meantime, in a 4-cup measuring cup (1L pitcher) , or medium mixing bowl, measure out the milk, maple syrup, and then add the eggs, cinnamon, ginger, salt and corn starch. Beat, using a fork or an immersion blender, until the ingredients are well combined.

3. When the pressure cooking time is up, open the cooker by releasing the pressure. Tumble the cooked butternut squash in a fine-mesh

strainer press on the squash pulp to release some liquid (save this liquid to use in place of stock in other recipes).

4. Measure the strained pumpkin pulp by jamming it into a 2-cup measure (or weighing out 550g) - Plop the pulp into the measuring cup with the egg mixture and blend well.

5. To make cute crust-less pies in the pressure cooker: Add 1 cup (250ml) water, or your pressure cooker's minimum liquid requirement, to the instant pot and steamer basket or trivet and set aside. Pour the mixture into heat-proof ramekins and lower into the instant pot un-covered - put the second layer on to of the first by balancing on the edges of the ramekins, below. Close and lock the lid of the pressure cooker.

6. Cook for 8-10 minutes at high pressure. When cooking time is up count 10 minutes of natural open time.

7. Then, release the rest of the pressure slowly using the valve. Lift the ramekins out of the pressure cooker using tongs and let stand 5 minutes before serving or let cool completely, cover tightly and refrigerate for up to two days.

Raspberry Chia Pudding

INGREDIENTS

16oz cultured cream cheese

2 large eggs

1medium vanilla bean, scraped

1 teaspoon organic vanilla extract

1/2 cup sugar

Red Raspberry Chia

INSTRUCTIONS

1. Combine all ingredients in your blend and blend until completely smooth (do not put in the whole vanilla bean, just scrape out the seeds and discard the rest)
2. Transfer to a 7 inch spring form pan and cover tightly with foil.
3. Place 2 cups of water in your instant pot then your rack or steamer insert.
4. Place your filled & foiled spring form pan on top of your rack and cook under (high or standard pressure) for 20 minutes.
5. Allow to depressurize naturally, Remove from instant pot and cool to room temperature for 30-60 minutes before chilling in the refrigerator for 1+ hours prior to serving.

Pina Colada Rice Pudding

INGREDIENTS

1 cup White Rice

1 1/2 cup Water

1 Tbsp Coconut Oil

1/4 tsp Salt

14 oz Can of Coconut Milk

1/2 cup Sugar

2 Eggs

1/2 C. Milk or Half and Half

1 tsp Vanilla Extract

Optional: 8 oz can of Pineapple Tidbits and Toasted Coconut

INSTRUCTIONS

1. In the Instant Pot, combine water, rice and coconut oil and select manual, high pressure for 5 minutes.
2. After the pot beeps (let the pressure release naturally) then open the lid and add the coconut milk and sugar to the pot.
3. In a separate bowl, beat the eggs, with milk and vanilla and then pour into the Instant Pot little by little stirring constantly while pouring.
4. Turn on the Saute function on the Instant Pot and continue to stir until the mixture is thickened and starts to boil.
5. At that time pour in the pineapple and mix one last time.
6. Pour into dishes and serve warm with whipped cream and/or toasted coconut.

AIR FRYER COOKBOOK

Recipes for all situations

By: Louis Laurent

CONTENTS

INTRODUCTION

The Air fryer has made a massive impact to the culinary scene for many households around the world. This revolutionary device is helping so many people improve their lives and health by eating cleaner and healthier with an Air fryer. The ability to enjoy all your favourite deep fried meals without the excess saturated fat and oil means managing your weight has never been easier. You no longer have to refrain yourself from fast food classics or eat smaller portions, because the Air fryer makes these classics healthier with less calories per bite.

Not only does the air fryer eradicate the need for large quantities of oil used for cooking, the elimination of cooking food in high temperature oil means you instantly decreased your chances of cancer. Cooking in hot oil has been well documented to be potentially carcinogenic, increasing an individual's possibility to develop cancer. The health benefits from cooking with an air fryer are huge, and makes it an obvious kitchen staple appliance.

Unfortunately, this fantastic device has been left collecting dust on many kitchen countertops, because of the lack of imagination and understanding on what this great device can actually do. An air fryer doesn't only replace your deep fryer in the kitchen, but also your oven and grill top!

It's potential is astonishing to any enthusiastic foodie or wannabe master chef, and this book aims to help you use your air fryer to its fullest potential. The recipes in this book will cover all the possible applications an air fryer can be used for and help you understand how classic dishes need to be adjusted for the air fryer to achieve the same results, if you were cooking the same dish without.

The primary aim of this book is to provide a solid foundation of air fryer recipes for your daily use to fit most situations, and also provide you enough experience and knowledge to begin experimenting and adjusting your own favourite meals to be cooked with an air fryer.

BREAKFAST RECIPES

English Fry Up

Serves: 4
Prep time: 2 mins
Cook time: 20 mins
Total time: 22 mins

Ingredients

8 Medium Sausages
8 Rashers Smoked Back Bacon
4 Eggs
1 Can Baked Beans
8 Slices Toast

Instructions

1. Place your sausages and bacon into the Air fryer and cook for 10 minutes on 300 F.

2. Place the baked beans in a ramekin dish

3. In another ramekin dish, crack your egg in (ready for it to be fried).

4. Cook for a further 10 minutes on 360 F until everything is cooked.

5. Pop your bread in the toaster while everything is being cooked in the air fryer.

6. Dish up and serve.

Notes:

A good English Fry up is a personal affair, so change the amount of bacon or add in hash browns etc to this recipe until you have your ultimate English Fry up.

Quick N Easy Breakfast Sandwich

Serves: 1
Prep time: 1 mins
Cook time: 6 mins
Total time: 7 mins

Ingredients

1 Large egg

1 English back bacon or 2 pieces of streaky bacons

1 English muffin

1 Pinch of pepper and salt

Instructions

1.   Crack the egg into an ramekin dish

2.   Place the egg, bacon and muffin into the air fryer at 390 F for 6
minutes

3.   Place your sandwich parts together and enjoy!

Sausage Frittata

Serves: 2
Prep time: 2 min
Cook time: 10 mins
Total time: 12 mins

Ingredients

3 Eggs

½ Italian sausage

4 Cherry tomatoes

1 tbp olive oil

Chopped parsley

Shredded cheese

Salt and Pepper to taste

Instructions

1. Preheat the air fryer to 360 F.

2. Chop your washed cherry tomatoes in half and sausage into small bite sized pieces.

3. Place the cherry tomatoes and sausage pieces into the baking pan and bake for 5 minutes.

4. At the same time, whisk the remaining ingredients together in a bowl.

5. Pour the mixture in, once the sausage meat is cooked, and bake for another 5 minutes.

Notes:

Use any cheese you like, but I advice on using shredded cheese so it melts evenly.

BIG Breakfast Burrito

Serves: 1
Prep time: 2 mins
Cook time: 10 mins
Total time: 12 mins

Ingredients

3-4 Slices of cooked Chicken Breast

2 Eggs

1/4 Red Bell Pepper, Sliced

1/4 Avocado, Sliced

1/8 Cup of Grated Mozzarella Cheese

2 tbsp Salsa

Pinch of Salt & Pepper

Tortilla

Instructions

1. Beat 2 eggs in a small bowl. Add salt and pepper to taste.

2. Pour the egg mixture into a small non-stick pan and place into the Air fryer basket.

Cook the egg in the Air fryer at 395 F for 5 minutes.

3. Then remove the pan from the air fryer and the egg from the pan.

4. Start filling your tortilla with the egg, sliced turkey or chicken breast, red pepper, avocado, cheese and salsa. Wrap it up, but make sure it's not over stuffed.

5. Line the Air fryer tray with tin foil and place the burrito on top. Heat up the burrito in the Air fryer at 350 F for 3 minutes so that the cheese melts and the tortilla gets nice and toasty.

Notes:
You can grill your red peppers in the air fryer by simply using the grilling pan after your eggs are done before wrapping your burrito.

Ham & Cheese Bread Cups

Serves: 2
Prep time: 2 mins
Cook time: 5 mins
Total time: 7 mins

Ingredients

2 Slices of sandwich bread

2 Medium eggs

2 Slices of sandwich ham

Shredded cheddar

Salt and pepper

Instructions

1. Preheat the air fryer at 360 F.
2. Wisk your eggs in a bowl
3. Cut your ham into small piece and place them into the egg mixture
4. Place a slice of bread into a muffin mould to make the bread cup.
5. Pour the egg ham mixture into the bread cups and sprinkle cheese on top.
6. Place the muffin mould into the air fryer at 360 F. for 5 min
7. Pop your bread cups out and add salt and pepper to taste.

Scrambled Eggs with Spinach

Serves: 2
Prep time: 1 mis
Cook time: 6 mins
Total time: 7 mins

Ingredients

2 Large eggs

100g Spinach

A knob of unsalted butter

Salt and pepper

Instructions

1. Place the baking pan into the air fryer and preheat the air fryer to 280 F.
2. Whisk the 2 eggs in a bowl and season with salt and pepper to taste
3. Melt the knob of butter in the baking pan and spread it all over the pan
4. Pour your egg mixture into the baking pan and stir the mixture every few minutes
5. Place your spinach in while your eggs are not fully cooked, and continue stirring until the eggs are fluffy and yellow.

French Toast Soldiers

Serves: 1
Prep time: 3 mins
Cook time: 10 mins
Total time: 13 mins

Ingredients

1 Slice of sandwich bread

1 Medium egg

Spreadable butter

Salt

Honey/ Syrup (optional)

Instructions

1. Preheat your air fryer at 360 F.
2. Spread butter onto your bread and cut your bread into finger width stripes
3. Beat your egg in a shallow bowl and season with salt
4. Dip your stripes of bread into the egg and place them into the air fryer for 4 minutes
5. Take the pan out and flip your bread soldiers over and place them back into the air fryer for another 4 minutes.
6. You will want to keep an eye on your bread soldiers to ensure you take them out once they are golden.
7. Serve with syrup or honey, or you can even dip them into your soft-boiled egg!

Apple Fritters

Serves: 1
Prep time: 10 mins
Cook time: 4 mins
Total time: 14 mins

Ingredients

2 Large tbsp of sugar

3/4 tsp ground cinnamon

Cooking oil sprays

½ cup gluten-free old-fashioned oats

3/8 tsp coarse salt

1 Egg

1 Large crisp apple, peeled, cored and sliced into ¼"-thick rings

Instructions

1. Whisk the sugar and cinnamon together.
2. Preheat your air fryer to 360 F.
3. Place your oats into a food processor and pulse the oats until a coarse powder.
4. Transfer your sugar cinnamon mix into a large bowl and mix the processed oats.
5. Beat your egg into a shallow pan.
6. Take your prepared apple slices and dip them into the egg. Once coated with sufficient egg, dip your apple into the dry mix.
7. Place your coated apple pieces into the air fryer at 360 for 4 minutes.

Blueberry Muffins

Serves: 6
Prep time: 5 mins
Cook time: 15 mins
 Total time: 20 mins

Ingredients

175g Sugar

250g Low fat yogurt

280g Flour

150g Blueberries

1 Egg

A few drops of vanilla essence

3 tsp baking powder

Instructions

1. Preheat your air fryer to 320 F.
2. Beat your egg and then add in the yogurt, vanilla essence and sugar, mix thoroughly
3. Add in the flour slowly as well as the baking powder.
4. Once the mix is thoroughly mixed, fold in the blueberries and fill your mix into muffin moulds.
5. Place your muffins into the air fryer at 320 F. for 15 minutes.

Bacon Baked Eggs

Serves: 2
Prep time: 2 mins
Cook time: 27 mins
Total time: 29 mins

Ingredients

2 Eggs

1 Slice bacon

2 tbsp milk or heavy cream

1 tsp vegan grated Parmesan cheese

1 tsp tomato or marinara sauce (optional)

½ tsp pepper

Instructions

1. Preheat your Air fryer to 360 F for 3 minutes.
2. Place bacon in and cook for 19 minutes. Cut into small pieces and divide the bacon pieces equally between two ramekins.
3. Crack an egg into each ramekin. Add a tablespoon of milk to each ramekin.
4. Season the egg with pepper.
5. Sprinkle 1 teaspoon of Parmesan cheese onto each ramekin. Cook for 8 minutes for a slightly runny yolk, and up to 10 minutes for a mostly hard yolk.

Notes:

You can add tomato paste to your ramekins before baking your eggs

Breakfast Soufflé

Serves: 2
Prep time: 2 mins
Cook time: 8 mins
Total time: 10 mins

Ingredients

2 Eggs

2 tbsp light cream

Red chili pepper

Parsley

Instructions

1. Finely chop the parsley and chilli. Use as much or as little as you wish.
2. Crack the eggs into a bowl and mix the cream in with the parsley and chilli
3. Pour your mixture into ramekin dishes and place them into your air fryer for 8 minutes at 400 F.

Notes:

If you want your soufflé to be soft, then 5 minutes instead of 8 should be used.

Cheese N Onion Omelette

Serves: 2
Prep time: 2 mins
Cook time: 12 mins
Total time: 14 mins

Ingredients

2 Eggs

1/4 Onion (medium - sliced)

Salt and Pepper to taste

Cheddar Cheese (grated)

Cooking Spray

Instructions

1. Dice your onion and place them into an oiled baking tray.
2. Place your onions into the air fryer for 8 minutes at 360 F.
3. Whisk your eggs and season with salt and pepper while your onions are in the air fryer.
4. Once your onions are soft, pour your egg mixture into the baking tray and sprinkle grated cheddar or any cheese of your choice on top.
5. Let the eggs cook for 4 minutes at 360 F.

Toasted Milk Buns

Serves: 2
Prep time: 5 mins
Cook time: 3 mins
Total time: 8 mins

Ingredients

2 Bread buns

1 Large egg

Evaporated milk

2 tbsp of sugar

Cooking oil

Instructions

1. Preheat your air fryer to 360 F for 5 minutes
2. Beat your egg in a shallow pan.
3. Cut your buns into half and dip the interior side into the egg.
4. Place your buns face up into your air fryer and cook for 3 minutes or until bun is toasted
5. Take your buns out and allow to cool.
6. Serve with a drizzle of evaporated milk and a sprinkle of sugar!

Bacon Onion Omelette

Serves: 2

Prep time: 2 mins

Cook time: 5 mins

Total time: 7 mins

Ingredients

4 Eggs

2 Slices of bacon

2 Small shallots

Instructions

1. Dice your shallots and slice your bacon into small pieces.

2. Beat your eggs and pour the mixture into an oiled backing tray.

3. Pour in your chopped ingredients in and cook for 5 minutes at 360 F.

Bombay Omelette

Serves: 2
Prep time: 4 mins
Cook time: 10 mins
Total time: 14 mins

Ingredients

½ Red onion
4 Cherry tomatoes
½ A bunch of fresh coriander
1 Green chilli
4 Large eggs
½ tsp ground turmeric
½ tsp garam masala
½ tsp ground cumin
2 Knobs of butter

Instruction

1. Finely chop the onion. Halve the cherry tomatoes and discard the seeds with a teaspoon, then finely slice the tomatoes.

2. Finely chop the coriander leaves. Halve the chilli, deseed and finely slice.

3. Whisk the eggs together until well combined, then season generously and whisk in the onion, tomatoes, coriander, chilli, turmeric, garam masala and cumin.

4. Set your air fryer to 360 F. Melt you butter in the baking pan and Swirl the eggs around for 10 minutes.

Ham n Egg Bread Bowls

Serves: 4
Prep time: 5 mins
Cook time: 10 mins
Total time: 15 mins

Ingredients

4 Lunch sized bread rolls

4 Slices of ham

4 Medium eggs

½ cup shredded mozzarella cheese

1 tbsp fresh parsley, finely chopped

Instructions

1. Preheat air fryer to 360F.
2. Cut the tops off the bread rolls, and Scoop out the centre
3. Line the bread bowl with a layer of ham. Try to use one whole piece if you can because then there is less chance of egg seeping through and being soaked up by the bread.
4. Crack in an egg.
5. Top each with 2 tbsp of mozzarella cheese and a sprinkle of parsley
6. Put the top back on each roll. Wrap with foil and place into the air fryer to bake for 10 to 15 minutes.

Baked Breakfast Potatoes

Serves: 2

Prep time: 1 min

Cook time: 50 mins

Total time: 51 mins

Ingredients

1/2 lb Baby Potatoes, cut into 1 inch chunks

2 TBS Vegetable oil

2 TBS Butter, melted

1 tsp Garlic powder

1 tsp Seasoning salt

2 Heaping tsp dried parsley

1 Medium onion, chopped

Salt and pepper to taste

Instructions

1. Preheat air fryer to 425 F.
2. Combine all ingredients in large bowl. Mix well to combine.
3. Spread out evenly into baking pan. Bake for 25 minutes, stirring once.
4. Turn heat up to 500 degrees.
5. Bake for 25 more minutes, stirring again before serving

Bacon Mashed Potato Cakes

Serves: 6
Prep time: 10 mins
Cook time: 6 mins
Total time: 16 mins

Ingredients

2 cups mashed potato, cold

1 Large egg

⅓ cup plain flour

1 cup grated cheese

8oz / 250g bacon, diced

½ cup scallions/shallots, thinly sliced

¼ tsp salt

2 cups breadcrumbs

4 to 6 tbsp oil (any cooking oil)

Pepper to taste

Instructions

1. Mix together the Potato Cake ingredients in a bowl until just combined.
2. Spread the breadcrumbs out on a large plate (to fit 6 patties).
3. Measure out ¼ cup level amount of potato mixture, and drop onto breadcrumbs. Repeat to fill plate, but leave sufficient space between the potato cakes.
4. Heat the air fryer to 360 F and oil the baking pan.
5. Cook the potato cakes on the baking pan by leaving them for 3 minutes until the down facing side is golden.
6. Then flip the potato cake to cook another 3 minutes.
7. Remove onto a paper towel lined baking tray.

Spinach Breakfast Puffs

Serves: 3
Prep time: 10 mins
Cook time: 20 mins
Total time: 30 mins

Ingredients

100g cream cheese, softened

1 Large egg

1 tbp olive oil

½ tsp. dried dill

2 cups of coarsely chopped spinach

¾ cup crumbled feta

2 tsp. bacon bits

Salt and pepper to taste

1 Sheet frozen puff pastry, thawed

1 tbp butter, melted

Instructions

1. Spray 9 cups in a muffin pan with cooking spray.
2. Microwave your cream cheese 10 seconds at a time until it's soft and melted but not steaming. Add egg, oil and dill into cream cheese and mix until well combined.
3. In a separate bowl combine spinach, feta and bacon. Pour your cream cheese mixture on top and season with salt and pepper. Stir together.
4. Cut pastry sheet into 9 squares. Line muffin pan with your cut squares (you might need to stretch them out a little). Press into the bottom of the muffin cups. Evenly divide the spinach mix among the cups. Bring your 4 pastry points together, covering the filling, and press them together. Lightly brush with the melted butter

5.   Bake at 400 F. about 20 minute until golden and puffy. Allow to cool for 10 minutes then use a knife around the edges to loosen and help pop them out.

Family Cheese N Bacon Baked Bread

Serves: 8
Prep time: 15 mins
Cook time: 30 mins
Total time: 45 mins

Ingredients

300g Bacon, diced

6 Eggs

1¼ cups milk

¼ tsp salt

Black pepper

7 cups Baguette : cut into 1 inch cubes (preferably slightly stale)

2 cups grated cheddar cheese

Parsley, finely chopped

Instructions

1.   Heat a large non stick pan over high heat. (Use a bit of oil if
     not using non stick). Add all but 2 tbsp of bacon (reserve for
     topping) and cooked until lightly browned. Remove from the fry
     pan and drain on a paper towel.

2.   Whisk the eggs, milk, salt and pepper in a bowl.

3.   Place the bread in a large ziplock bag. Pour in the egg mixture,
     1½ cups cheese and cooked bacon (reserve the uncooked bacon).
     Seal and massage the egg into the cubes. Set aside in the fridge
     for at least 30 minutes (until all the egg is soaked into the bread)
     or overnight.

To Cook

1. Preheat Air fryer to 350F.

2. Spray the baking pan. Pour the bread mixture into the cake tin, pat down to compress and scatter with remaining uncooked bacon and remaining ½ cup cheese. Cover loosely with foil or with a pan lid.

3. Bake for 25 minutes, then remove the lid and bake for a further 10 minutes until bubbly and golden on top.

4. Allow to rest for 5 minutes before removing the spring form and cutting into slices to serve. Garnish with parsley if using.

Baked Avocado

Serves: 1
Prep time: 3 mins
Cook time: 15 mins
Total time: 18 mins

Ingredients

1 Large avocado

2 Eggs

1 Slice of smoked bacon

Instructions

1. Preheat air fryer to 420 F.
2. Halve the avocado and remove the pit
3. Cave a little further from the avocado egg so that it fits well
4. Place the avocado halves in a baking dish
5. Break in each half of the avocado egg
6. Sprinkle with salt and pepper
7. Cut the bacon into small pieces and spread over the avocado
8. Turn is about fifteen minutes in the oven until the egg coagulated and cooked

Raisin Muffins

Serves: 6
Prep time: 5 mins
Cook time: 15 mins
Total time: 20 mins

Ingredients

½ cup all-purpose flour

1 tbsp baking powder

3 tbsp brown sugar

1 Small egg

½ cup rolled oats

½ cup raisins

½ cup semi-skimmed milk

Salt to taste

Instructions

1. Preheat air fryer to 400 F.
2. Take a large bowl and mix the flour, baking powder, brown sugar, oats and salt.
3. Whisk the egg and milk in another bowl and slowly stir the mixture with the dry ingredients of the other bowl.
4. Pour in the raisins and stir into the muffin mix.
5. Fill your muffin mix into muffin cups or a muffin tray and place them into the air fryer for 15 minutes or until golden brown.

Crispy Chicken Wraps

Serves: 4
Prep time: 7 mins
Cook time: 12 mins
Total time: 19 mins

Ingredients

2 tbsp Olive oil

1 cup golden breadcrumbs

1 Medium egg

1lb Chicken tenderloins

½ tsp salt

Black pepper to taste

Whole grain burrito wraps

Greek yoghurt

Fresh Mint

Salad Mix

Instructions

1. Preheat the air fryer at 360 F.

2. Whisk your egg in a shallow pan and place your breadcrumbs onto a large plate.

3. Mix the Olive oil into the breadcrumbs until the Olive oil has been evenly distributed.

4. Season your breadcrumb mix with salt and pepper to taste.

5. Dip your chicken tenderloins into the egg first, and then the breadcrumbs second.

6. Place your chicken into the air fryer basket and cook for 12 minutes

until your breadcrumbs are golden yellow.

7. While your chicken is cooking, grab your fresh mint and coarsely chop the mint leaves and mix into the yoghurt.

8. Once your chicken is cooked, take your chicken out from the air fryer to cool.

9. Lay a wrap down and spread a tablespoon of yoghurt and place a chicken tenderloin with some salad greens on top.

10. Wrap and enjoy!

Pancakes

Serves: 2
Prep time: 5 mins
Cook time: 8 mins
Total time: 13 mins

Ingredients

1 ½ cups all purpose flour

3 tbsp of maple syrup

2 Medium eggs

½ cup semi-skimmed milk

Cooking oil

Instructions

1. Preheat the air fryer to 360 F.

2. Mix all ingredients in a large bowl.

3. Lightly oil your baking pan and pour in ¼ inch thick of pancake batter in.

4. Cook for 3 minutes before flipping to cook for another 5 minutes, or flip until the edges of your pancake have changed colour.

5. Repeat until all the batter has been cooked.

Hash Browns

Serves: 1
Prep time: 5 mins
Cook time: 16 mins
Total time: 21 mins

Ingredients

1 cup diced potato
1 tbsp Olive oil
Salt and pepper to taste

Instructions

1. Preheat air fryer to 360 F.

2. Place your potatoes into a bowl and evenly coat your potatoes with Olive oil.

3. Season your potatoes with salt and pepper to taste.

4. Place your potatoes into the air fryer to cook for 16 minutes, or until golden brown.

Note:

If you want your hash browns to be crispy then don't touch or stir them while they cook! And instead let them cook for 10 minutes before flipping the potatoes in one go and cook for another 5 minutes.

LUNCH RECIPES

Stuffed Tomatoes

Serves: 3
Prep time: 12 mins
Cooked time 25 mins
Total time: 37 mins

Ingredients

3 Large tomatoes

2 cups white cooked rice

1 Medium onion, diced

1 Medium carrot diced

1 Minced garlic clove

Salt, pepper and cumin to taste

Instructions

1. Heat a frying pan and spray an appropriate amount of cooking oil. Saute the carrots, onions and garlic for 3 minutes. Season the medley to taste with salt, pepper and cumin powder.

2. Place your medley into a bowl and mix in the cooked rice.

3. Preheat the air fryer to 340 F.

4. Cut the tops of your tomatoes and place them to the side.

5. Scoop the seeds out of the tomatoes and fill them with your rice mix. Place the tops back on and the tomatoes into the air fryer. Let it cook for 20 minutes.

Lemon & Garlic Chicken Drumsticks

Serves: 2
Prep time: 3 mins
Cook time: 20 mins
Total time: 23 mins

Ingredients

1lb Chicken drumsticks

Fresh coriander leaves

1 tbsp chopped garlic

3 tbsp lemon juice

1 tbsp cooking oil

Salt and pepper to taste

Instructions

1. Preheat air fryer to 380 F.

2. Chop your coriander leaves.

3. Place all your ingredients into a bowl and mix. Ensure the chicken is evenly coated with the garlic, lemon juice and coriander leaves.

4. Place your chicken into the air fryer and cook for 20 minutes.

Mushroom & Onion Frittatas

Serves: 4
Prep time: 10 mins
Cook time: 20 mins
Total time: 30 mins

Ingredients

2 cups Sliced mushrooms of your choice

1 tbp Olive oil

½ Red onion

8 Medium eggs

Salt to taste

Crumbled Feta

Instructions

1. Cut your Red Onion and mushroom into thin slices around the same thickness.

2. Sweat the onions and mushrooms in a pan until tender for 5 minutes.

3. Place the onions and mushrooms on a plate and use a kitchen towel to pat dry the excess moisture.

4. Preheat the air fryer to 360 F.

5. Crack your eggs into a big bowl and whisk.

6. Lightly oil your ramekin dishes and pour enough egg to fill ¾ of each dish. Then place ¼ of the dish with your onions, mushrooms and cheese.

7. Place your ramekin dishes into the air fryer and cook for 15 minutes.

Note:

Stick a knife into your frittata and if the knife comes out clean then they are ready to eat!

Crab Cakes

Serves: 4
Prep time: 15 mins
Cook time: 10 mins
Total time: 25 mins

Ingredients

½ lb Cooked crab meat

½ lb Cooked white fish meat

2 cups of chunky or smooth mash potato

¼ cup skim milk

1 Egg

1 cup Breadcrumbs

1 cup all purpose flour

Parsley

Chive

Salt and pepper to taste

Instructions

1. Place your breadcrumbs onto a place and your flour on to another plate.

2. Crack your egg into a shallow dish and beat thoroughly.

3. Take a handful of parsley and chive and chop coarsely and place into a large bowl.

4. Place your mashed potato in with your herbs and season with salt and pepper to taste.

5. Then mix in your crab and fish meat into your mash potatoes and season again.

6. Preheat air fryer to 360 F.

7. With your hands, grab a handful of your crab cake and roll into a ball.

8. Once into a ball, gently shaped your crab cake into a 2 inch thick cylinder.

9. Coat your crab cake into flour by rolling it once, then dip your crab cake in the egg and proceed to coat your crab cake into the breadcrumbs by rolling it once.

10. Do this until you have no more crab cake mix left.

11. Then place your crab cakes into the air fryer and cook for 10 minutes or until the breadcrumbs have turned golden.

Stuffed Bell Peppers with Quinoa

Serves: 4
Prep time: 4 mins
Cook time: 10 mins
Total time: 14 mins

Ingredients

4 Large bell peppers

2 cups cooked Quinoa

1 Diced red Onion

¼ Chopped parsley

¼ Chopped cashews

Salt and pepper to taste

Olive oil

Instructions

1. Preheat the air fryer to 400 F.

2. Cut the top of each Bell pepper and set the top aside.

3. Mix the Quinoa, Onion, parsley and cashews in a bowl, season to taste and drizzle a little Olive oil to help cook the onions later.

4. Fill each bell pepper with your quinoa mix and place the tops back on.

5. Place your Bell peppers into the air fryer to cook for 10 minutes.

Chicken Schnitzel

Serves: 1
Prep time: 5 mins
Cook time: 8 mins
Total time: 13 mins

Ingredients

1 Boneless chicken breast

2 tbsp all purpose flour

1 Egg

4 tbsp breadcrumbs

Salt and black pepper to taste

Instructions

1. Preheat air fryer to 360 F.

2. Take your chicken breast and flatten it with a meat tenderiser until it's ½ inch thick.

3. Season the chicken with salt and pepper.

4. Crack your egg into a bowl and beat it lightly, transfer your egg into a dish.

5. Place your breadcrumbs onto a plate.

6. Dip the chicken into the egg mix and then again into the breadcrumbs. Ensure your chicken is well coated with breadcrumbs.

7. Place your chicken into the air fryer to cook for 8 minutes or until the breadcrumbs are golden.

Korean Chicken Wings

Serves: 4
Prep time: 35 mins
Cook time: 15 mins
Total time: 50 mins

Ingredients

2 lbs Chicken wings

4 Garlic cloves pressed

3 tbsp soy sauce

2 Thin slices of ginger

1 tbsp white vinegar

Sugar to taste

Instructions

1. Take your ginger slices and finely cut them into thing stripes.

2. Mix your ginger, garlic, soy sauce and vinegar together. Add a sprinkle of sugar to cut the tartness.

3. Marinate your chicken wings with your sauce for 30 minutes in the fridge.

4. Take your chicken wings out and place them into your air fryer at 400 F. Cook for 15 minutes.

Teriyaki Chicken Skewers

Serves: 2
Prep time: 10 mins
Cook time: 10 mins
Total time: 20 mins

Ingredients

3 tbsp Teriyaki sauce

½ lb Chicken breast meat

½ tp Ground black pepper

4 Thin slice of ginger

Instructions

1. Cut your chicken breast into ½ inch chucks, and skewer them onto a wooden kebab stick. Place your ginger slices in between chunks.

2. Season your chicken with ground black pepper.

3. Place your chicken skewers into the air fryer at 360 F.

4. Brush on a thin layer of teriyaki sauce onto your chicken every few minutes until fully cooked.

Falafel

Serves: 2

Prep time: 10 mins

Cook time: 15 mins

Total time: 25 mins

Ingredients

250ml Tin chick peas

½ Diced onion

2 garlic cloves

Coriander leaves

1 tbsp garam masala

Salt to taste

1. **Instructions**

2. Add all ingredients into a food processor and pulse until all is mixed thoroughly and the chick peas are coarse.

3. Oil your hands and then proceed to make falafel balls from the mix.

4. Place your falafels into the air fryer at 400 F. to cook for 15 minutes.

Tuna Stuffed Roast Potato

Serves: 1
Prep time: 5 mins
Cook time: 30 mins
Total time: 35 mins

Ingredients

1 Potato big enough for a baked potato serving

1 tbsp Olive oil

1 tbsp of unsalted butter

Half a tin of Tuna (50ml)

3 tbsp Mayonnaises

Salt and pepper to taste

Instructions

1. Preheat air fryer to 350 F.

2. Peel and wash your potato.

3. Make thin cuts into the potato about 1 inch deep or halfway down the potato. Do this for the entire length of the potato.

4. Lightly coat your potato with Olive oil and season with salt and pepper.

5. Place your potato into the Air fryer to cook for 30 – 45 minutes depending on the size of your potato.

6. While the potato is cooking; mix the mayonnaise and tuna in a bowl. Ensure the tuna is not too chunky.

7. Take the potato out once cooked and add the butter and tuna on top.

Stuffed Mushrooms

Serves: 1
Prep time: 2 mins
Cook time: 10 mins
Total time: 12 mins

Ingredients

3 Large portabello mushrooms

3 tbsp Pesto

3 tbsp Mozzarella cheese

Instructions

1. Preheat air fryer to 360 F

2. Wash your mushrooms and pat dry with a kitchen towel.

3. Cut the mushroom stalks and fill each mushroom with 1 tablespoon of pesto and 1 tablespoon of cheese.

4. Place the mushrooms into the air fryer to cook for 10 minutes.

Chicken Parmesan

Serves: 2
Prep time: 1 min
Cook time: 12 mins
Total time: 13 mins

Ingredients

2 Boneless chicken breast

1 cup shredded mozzarella cheese

½ cup tomato sauce

Instructions

1. Preheat air fryer to 400 F for 5 minutes

2. Place the chicken breasts in the air fryer and brush a layer of tomato sauce on the chicken after 5 minutes of cooking. Leave the chicken to cook for another 5 minutes.

3. Take your chicken out and sprinkle the cheese on top. Place the chicken back in the air fryer for another 2 minutes.

Swedish Meatballs

Serves: 3
Prep time: 5 mins
Cook time: 18 mins
Total time: 23 mins

Ingredients

¼ Ground beef

¼ Ground pork

1 Egg

Salt and pepper to taste

Instructions

1. Preheat air fryer to 360 F

2. Mix the meat and egg in a large bowl until all ingredients are well combined

3. Season you meat with salt and pepper and male 1 inch thick meatballs.

4. Place the meatballs in the air fryer to cook for 18 minutes

Note:

Your ground meat should be 70% lean and 30% fat to achieve a firm but juicy texture.

Spicy Potato Wedges

Serves: 4
Prep time: 5 mins
Cook time: 15 mins
Total time: 20 mins

Ingredients

4 Medium sized potatoes

¼ tsp salt

¼ tsp ground black pepper

½ tsp paprika

Chilli flakes to taste

Instructions

1. Wash your potatoes and cut them into wedges.

2. Place your salt, pepper, paprika and chilli flakes in a large bowl and mix.

3. Place your potato wedges into the bowl and ensure every wedge is evenly coated.

4. Place your air fryer at 500 F and cook for 15 minutes.

Tortellini Veggie Soup

Serves: 4
Prep time: 5 mins
Cook time: 25 mins
Total time: 30 mins

Ingredients

½ cup dried tortellini

1 Diced carrot

 1 Finely chopped onions

½ Diced courgettes

¼ Chopped leek

3 cups vegetable stock

Salt and pepper to taste

Croutons

Instructions

1. Place all ingredients into the air fryer to 360 F and cook until boiling. Check ever 5 minutes.

2. Turn the air fryer down to 260 F to simmer for 5 minutes.

Mac N Cheese

Serves: 1
Prep time: 5 mins
Cook time: 15 mins
Total time: 20 mins

Ingredients

1 cup Cooked macaroni

½ cup warmed milk

1 ½ cup grated cheddar cheese

3 tbsp Parmesan cheese

1 Bacon rasher

Salt and pepper to taste

Instructions

1. Preheat air fryer to 400 F

2. Place your cooked macaroni into the backing pan and mix in the cheddar cheese and season.

3. Sprinkle the Parmesan cheese on top and pour the warm milk evenly onto your macaroni.

4. Place your baking tray into the air fryer to cook for 15minutes.

Salmon Fillet

Serves: 1
Prep time: 2 mins
Cook time: 10 mins
Total time: 12 mins

Ingredients

1 Salmon fillet

Salt and pepper to taste

Olive oil

Instructions

1. Preheat air fryer to 340 F

2. Season the salmon fillet with salt and pepper.

3. Lightly brush the salmon fillet with Olive oil on the meat side and leave the skin side un-oiled.

4. Place your salmon into the air fryer to cook for 10 – 15 minutes depending on the thickness of the salmon.

Baked Avocado

Serves: 2
Prep time: 3 mins
Cook time: 8 mins
Total time: 11 mins

Ingredients

1 Large avocado

1 Egg

Salt and ground black pepper to taste

Instructions

1. Cut the Avocado length ways and discard the stone.

2. Whisk your egg in a bowl and pour the mixture into the avocado halves where the stone use to be.

3. Place your avocado halves into the air fryer at 360 F for 8 minutes.

4. Finish by seasoning before serving.

Note:

A ripe avocado that is still firm works best for this recipe.

Sausage Rolls

Serves: 1
Prep time: 10 mins
Cook time: 10 mins
Total time: 20 mins

Ingredients

Thawed Puff pastry sheet

2 Sausages of your choice

1 Lightly beaten egg

2 tbsp melted butter

Instructions

1. Preheat air fryer to 500 F

2. Lay the puff pastry flat on a counter and brush the melted butter all over the puff pastry.

3. Lay your sausages along the middle of the puff pastry.

4. Bring opposite sides of the pastry together and use a fork to seal the two ends together by pressing down along the length of the pastry.

5. Use a brush to coat the top of your sausage roll with egg.

6. Cut the sausage roll into four equal pieces and place them into the air fryer to cook for 10 minutes.

Mini Calzones

Serves: 4
Prep time: 5 mins
Cook time: 10 mins
Total time: 15 mins

Ingredients

300g Pizza dough

4 tbsp Tomato sauce

4 tbsp Parmesan cheese

4tbsp Mozzarella cheese

1/3 cup sliced mushrooms

½ Italian seasoning

1 Clove garlic pressed

¼ Sliced Italian sausage

½ Sliced red onion

1 Egg lightly beaten

Instructions

1. Preheat air fryer to 500 F.

2. Place tomato sauce, cheeses, mushroom, onion, garlic, sausage meat and seasoning in a large bowl; mix well.

3. Divide your pizza dough into 4 equal pieces and roll the dough out into ¼ inch thick circles.

4. Spoon the calzone filling onto half of the dough's surface, making sure to leave at least ½ inch gap from the edge.

5. Fold the other side of the pizza dough over and seal the ends with a

fork by pressing along the edges.

6. Use a brush to coat the top of your calzones with egg.

7. Place your calzones into the air fryer for 10 minutes or until golden.

DINNER RECIPES

Easy Salmon Steaks

Serves: 4
Prep time: 10mins
Cook time: 10mins
Total time: 20mins

Ingredients

4 Salmon steaks

4 Garlic cloves

3 tbsp Dijon Mustard

2 tbsp Fresh Lime juice

¼ cup Olive Oil

Salt and pepper to taste

Instructions

1. Preheat air fryer to 360 F.

2. Finely chop or press your garlic cloves and place them into a bowl.

3. Mix the Olive oil, Mustard, Lime juice, salt and pepper with the pressed garlic. Mix until all ingredients are well combined.

4. Use 1 tablespoon of sauce to marinate your salmon steaks. Use your hands to ensure the sauce is evenly coated.

5. Place your Salmon steaks into the air fryer to cook for 5 minutes. Turn your steaks over to cook for another 5 minutes.

6. Plate your Salmon steaks and drizzle the sauce on top for extra flavour.

Italian Pork Tenderloins

Serves: 4
Prep time: 5 mins
Cook time: 20 mins
Total time: 25 mins

Ingredients

1 ½ lbs Pork Tenderloin

½ tbp Black pepper

1 tbp Italian Seasoning mix

2 tbsp Olive oil

Salt to taste

Instructions

1. Preheat air fryer to 400 F.

2. Mix the Olive oil with the Black pepper, Italian spices and a pinch of salt in a dish.

3. Make incisions evenly spaced out by stabbing your pork tenderloin with a kitchen knife. You should have no more than 5-6 incisions at an inch deep.

4. Rub the spice mix onto your pork tenderloin.

5. Place your pork tenderloin into the baking pan and then to the air fryer, cook for 20 minutes.

6. **Note:**

7. Preparing your pork at room temperature make the end result taste better! You can also cut the cooking time by cutting your pork tenderloin into sections.

Crunchy Pork Cutlet

Serves: 4
Prep time: 3 mins
Cook time: 15 mins
Total time: 18 mins

Ingredients

1lb Pork cutlets

½ cup Breadcrumbs

1 tps Brown sugar

½ tps Paprika powder

½ tps Onion salt

1 tp Dijon mustard

Instructions

1. Preheat air fryer to 460 F.

2. Mix the brown sugar, paprika powder and onion salt into a small dish and rub the mixture onto your pork evenly.

3. Take your mustard and spread it onto your pork before dipping your pork into the breadcrumbs.

4. Place your pork into the air fryer to cook for 10 – 15 minutes depending on the thickness of your cutlets.

Cajun Shrimp

Serves: 4
Prep time: 5 mins
Cook time: 5 mins
Total time: 10 mins

Ingredients

1lb Tiger Shrimp

1 tbp Olive oil

¼ tsp smoked paprika

¼ tsp cayenne pepper

Salt to taste

Instructions

1. Preheat the air fryer to 360 F

2. Mix all the ingredients except for the tiger shrimp in a bowl.

3. Place your de-shelled shrimp in the bowl and coat your shrimp with the spices evenly.

4. Put the shrimp in the air fryer to cook for 5 minutes.

Fish N Chips

Serves: 8
Prep time: 15 mins
Cook time: 35 mins
Total time: 50 mins

Ingredients

Fish:
400 gm firm white fish fillet
2 Large eggs
1/2 cup plain flour
1/2 cup fresh bread crumbs
2 tbsp fresh parsley, chopped
1 tbsp olive oil
1 tsp salt
1 tsp freshly ground pepper

Chips:
2 Large potatoes, washed and scrubbed
1 tsp fresh rosemary
1 tbsp olive oil
2 Cloves garlic, crushed

Instructions

1. Preheat the Air fryer at 400 F for 5 minutes. Meanwhile, mix bread crumbs, salt, pepper, parsley and olive oil in a bowl.

2. Cut the fish into 8 long pieces. Crack the egg in a shallow bowl and use a fork to lightly whisk. Place the flour and breadcrumbs in separate shallow bowls.

3. Dip 1 piece of fish in the flour. Shake off any excess. Dip the fish in the egg, then in breadcrumbs, pressing firmly to coat.

4. Place the fish in air fryer. Repeat with all the remaining fish pieces and put in air fryer and cook for about 15 minutes or until golden.

5. For chips, cut the potatoes in wedges shape with skin on. Soak them in

a bowl with mild salted water for 20 minutes.

6. Preheat the air fryer at 360 F for 5 minutes. Drain the potatoes and pat them dry with a paper towel. In a bowl, mix all the ingredients along with potatoes and toss to coat evenly. Place the chips in air fryer and cook for 25 minutes until golden, shaking them once in between. Once cooked, toss the potatoes generously with salt.

7. For tartar sauce, mix all the ingredients in a bowl and chill in fridge until needed. Serve with fish and chips.

Roast Lamb Chops

Serves: 2
Prep time: 2 hours
Cook time: 18 mins
Total time: 2hrs 18mins

Ingredients

2 Lamb forequarter chops
Fresh rosemary
3 Cloves garlic, crushed
Black pepper
Salt

Instructions

1. Marinate lamb chops with salt, pepper, garlic and rosemary for 2-3 hours in the fridge.

2. Remove lamb chops from the fridge and place at room temperature 20 minutes before cooking.

   Air fry at 460 F for 18 minutes, flipping the lamb chops halfway through.

Honey Lime Chicken Wings

Serves: 4
Prep time: 6 hours
Cook time: 12 mins
Total time: 6 hrs 12 mins

Ingredients

16 mid joint chicken wings

Marinate

2 tbsp light soya sauce
2 tbsp good quality honey
1/2 tsp sea salt
1/4 tsp white pepper powder
1/2 crush black pepper
2 tbsp lime/ lemon juice

Instructions

1. Wash the mid wings, pat dry with kitchen towel.

2. Pour all marinates into a glass dish, add in mid wings, mix well and let it season for at least 6 hours if you don't have time, 1 day will be better. Cover with lip and refrigerate them.

3. Bring out to rest in room temperature for 30 mins before air frying.

4. Air fry the wings with 360 F for 6 mins, flip over 360 F for 6 mins and flip again.

5. Let it cool for 5 mins, serve with a wedge of lime/ lemon.

Note:

Watch out for the last 3 mins, it might burn easily because of the honey.

Sweet N Sour Pork

Serves: 4
Prep time: 15 mins
Cook time: 20 mins
Total time: 35 mins

Ingredients

1 Serving slice of fresh pineapple, cut in cubes

1 Medium size onion, sliced

1 Medium size tomato, cut in cubes

1 tbsp minced garlic

2 tbsp oyster sauce

2 tbsp of tomato sauce

1 tbsp of worchestire sauce

Sugar to taste

Plain flour

1 Egg

Instructions

Heat up the Air fryer at 240 F for 5 mins

When ready, dip pork in egg and then coat with plain flour.

Dust off any excess flour on the pork before placing into the frying basket.

Set timer to 20 minutes.

When it's done, set the meat aside to prepare the sauce.

Preparation of sauce:

With about a tsp of oil, fry garlic and onions till fragrant before adding tomatoes, pineapple

Add the oyster sauce, tomato sauce, worchestire sauce and stir

Add the cornflour and water to the sauce to thicken

Add the cooked pork cubes into the pan and coat it well with the sauce

Add sugar to taste, ensuring there's enough of the 'sweet' to the sourness of the sauce

Kentucky Fried Chicken

Serves: 6
Prep time: 10 mins
Cook time: 20 mins
Total time: 30 mins

Ingredients

2 Egg whites

100g Flour

1 tbsp Brown sugar

1 tbsp Salt

2tl (smoked) paprika powder

1 tsp onion powder

1 tsp garlic powder

1 tsp dried oregano

1 tsp dried basil

1 / 2tsp chili powder

1 / 2tsp black pepper

1 / 2tsp garlic powder

1 / 2tsps allspice powder

12 Chicken drumsticks

Instructions

1. Beat the egg whites separately and place ready in a deep plate.

2. Mix the flour with the sugar and salt and stir all the spices and seasoning, it also sets ready in a deep plate.

3. Coat each drumstick with the seasoning mix. Ensure that the whole drum stick is covered with a thick layer.

4. Put all the drumsticks on a plate and let them have "dry up" about 10 minutes.

5. Preheat your Air fryer to 400 F. Cook the drumsticks (preferably 6 pieces for a delicious crispy layer around) for 10 minutes at 400 F and then 10 minutes at 300 F for proper further cooking.

Tandoori Chicken

Serves: 4
Prep time: 15 mins
Cook time: 30 mins
Total time: 45 mins

Ingredients

4 Chicken leg (With Thigh)

For the first Marinade:

3 tsp Ginger paste

3 tsp Garlic paste

Salt to taste

3 tbsp Lemon juice

For the second Marinade

2 tbspTandoori masala powder

1 tsp Roasted cumin powder

1 tsp Garam masala powder

2 tsp Red chili powder

1 tsp Turmeric powder

4 tbsp Hung curd

1 tsp Black pepper powder

2 tsp Coriander powder

Instructions

1. Wash the chicken legs and make slits in them using a sharp knife.

2. Add chicken in a bowl along with the ingredients for the first marinade.

3. Mix well and keep aside for 15 minutes.

4. Mix the ingredients for the second marinade and pour them over the chicken.

5. Mix well.

6. Cover the bowl and refrigerate for at least 10-12 hours.

7. Line the basket of the air fryer with aluminium foil.

8. Preheat to 450 F.

9. Place the chicken on the basket and air fry for 18-20 minutes, until slightly charred and browned.

10. Serve hot with Yogurt mint dip and Onion rings.

Thai style Mussels

Serves: 2
Prep time: 5 mins
Cook time: 10 mins
Total time: 15 mins

Ingredients

500g mussels

2tbsp curry powder

Salt to taste

150ml Coconut milk

½ Stalk fresh Lemon grass

½ cup Parsley

2 Cloves of garlic

Instructions

1. Preheat air fryer to 360 F for 3 minutes.

2. Place the lemon grass, parsley and garlic in the air fryer.

3. Sprinkle the curry powder over the herbs.

4. Place your cleaned mussels on top of your herbs.

5. Cook for 5 minutes and stir.

6. Pour in the coconut milk and stir the mussels, cook for another 5 minutes.

Roast Beef Roll

Serves: 4
Prep time: 10 mins
Cook time: 15 mins
Total time: 25 mins

Ingredients

2 lbs Beef flank steak

3 tbsp Pesto

6 Slice Provolone cheese

3 oz. red bell peppers, roasted

1/3 cup baby spinach, fresh

1 tsp Sea Salt

1 tsp black pepper

Instructions

1. Open up (butter y) the steak. Spread the pesto evenly on the meat.

2. Layer the cheese, roasted red peppers & spinach 3/4 of the way down the meat.

3. Roll up and secure with toothpicks. Season with sea salt & pepper.

4. Place the roll ups in the Fry Basket and into the Air Fryer, cook for 14 minutes at 400 F.

5. Half way through, rotate the meat.

6. When done, let rest 10 minutes before cutting and serving.

Air fried Calamari

Serves: 2
Prep time: 15 mins
Cook time: 13 mins
Total time: 28 mins

Ingredients

1/2 lb Calamari tubes (tentacles if you prefer)

1 cup of club soda

1 cup Flour

A couple dashes of salt, red pepper and black pepper

½ tsp Paprika

Instructions

1. Rinse your calamari clean and blot dry.

2. Slice the calamari tubes into rings about 1/4 inch wide.

3. Place the calamari rings into a bowl and cover them with the club soda, stir until all are submerged. Let sit for 10 minutes.

4. Meanwhile combine the flour, salt, red & black pepper. Set aside. Drain the calamari, blot dry.

5. Dredge the calamari, one at a time, in the flour mixture and set on a plate until ready to air fry.

6. Spray the basket of the fryer with a small amount of cooking spray. Place calamari into the basket at 375 F for 11 minutes.

7. Shake the basket twice during the cooking process, loosening any rings that stick.

8. Remove from basket, toss with the sauce and return to the fryer for 2 minutes more.

Perfect Steak

Serves: 1
Prep time: 1 hour
Cook time:
Total time:

Ingredients

1 Skirt steak

1 Chipotle pepper (canned in adobo sauce)

1 tbsp adobo sauce

1/2 cup fresh cilantro, loosely packed

2 Cloves garlic

1 tsp cumin

1 Tbsp Chili powder

1 tsp salt

3 tbsp extra virgin olive oil

3 tbsp red wine vinegar

Instructions

1. Add all ingredients except for the steak into a blender or food processor. Blend until the whole mixture comes together.

2. Pour the mixture over the steak, coating on both sides, in a dish or plastic bag.

3. Allow to marinate for 1 hour at the least, but you can go as long as overnight.

4. When done marinating, grill steak in air fryer for 5 minutes at 360 F Skirt. steak can be tough if cooked incorrectly so be sure to se the above time as a guide only.

Grilled Tomatoes

Serves: 2
Prep time: 5 mins
Cook time: 20 mins
Total time: 25 mins

Ingredients

2 Tomatoes

Italian Herb Mix

Ground black pepper to taste

Instructions

1. Wash tomatoes. Cut in half and turn over. Spray bottoms lightly with 1 spray of cooking spray.

2. Turn all halves cut side up. Spray lightly with 1 spray of cooking spray.

3. Sprinkle with ground black pepper and Italian herb mix.

4. Place tomato halves into the air fryer for 20 minutes at 300 F, or until tomatoes reach the desired softness.

SIDES RECIPES

Pot Stickers

Serves: 4
Prep time: 10 mins
Cook time: 10 mins
Total time: 20 mins

Ingredients

3tbsp Water

30 Wonton wrappers

2 tsp Soy sauce

2 tbsp Cocktail sauce

1 Egg, lightly beaten

2 Finely chopped green onions

½ cup Chopped cabbage

½ lb Minced pork

Instructions

1. Mix the soy sauce, cocktail sauce, egg, green onion cabbage and minced pork together.
2. Place a wonton wrapper in one hand and spoon a tablespoon's worth of pot sticker filling in the middle. Bring one side of the wonton wrapper to the opposite site and seal the edge by crimping.
3. Place your pot stickers in a slightly oiled baking pan and cook for 10 minutes at 360 degrees F in your airfryer.

Samosa

Serves: 4
Prep time: 30 mins
Cook time: 15 mins
Total time: 45 mins

Ingredients

¾ cup boiled and blended Spinach

¼ cup green peas (small)

½ tsp Sesame seeds

2 tsp Cooking oil

1 tsp fresh coriander leaves, chopped

1 tsp Garam masala

¼ cup boil and diced potatoes

1 ½ cup all purpose flour

½ tsp Bicarbonate soda

Salt, chilli powder, chaat masala, white pepper to taste

Instructions

1. Make the dough by combining bicarbonate soda, salt and flour together. Once the dough begins to come together, add in 1 tablespoon of oil and knead the dough until it is smooth. Let it sit in the fridge for 20 minutes.

2. As the dough is resting, cook your diced potato and peas in a pan on low heat with the rest of the oil for 5 minutes. Once the peas and potatoes are soft, add in the sesame seeds, coriander and other spices in. Once the spices have been properly mixed in and its flavours are

becoming stronger, mix in the blended spinach. You will want to reduce your samosa filling on low heat so it is not too wet.

3. Once the filling is of appropriate wetness, take it off the stove and let it rest on the side.

4. Bring your dough back out to start kneading it into individual samosa portions. Make 1.5 inch size dough balls and roll each dough ball into thin rectangles.

5. Place the somasa wrapper flat on a surface, with the shorter side in front of you. Spoon in two tablespoon's worth of filling from the left corner nearest to you; forming a right angle triangle shape with the filling.

6. Bring the right corner nearest to you and fold up to cover the filling. Seal the edge with a fork and then carry on folding in triangles until there is no more wrapper to fold.

7. Preheat airfryer to 180 degrees F and allow your samosas to cook for 10 minutes or until the wrapper is golden.

Chunky Chips

Serves: 1
Prep time: 1 hour
Cook time: 10 mins
Total time: 1 hr 10 mins

Ingredients

1 Large potato

Instructions

1. Peel and chop your potato into 1 inch wide chips.
2. Soak your chips in a bowl of cold water with salt for 1 hour.
3. Drain your chips off on a kitchen towel.
4. Preheat airfryer to 360 degrees F. for 5 minutes.
5. Place your chips in the airfryer and allow to cook for 10 minutes or until slightly golden.

Banana Chips

Serves: 4
Prep time: 5 mins
Cook time: 10min
Total time: 15mins

Ingredients

Four bananas (raw)

Salt and pepper to taste

Instructions

1. Peel the Banana and slice them in the form of thin chips
2. Mix the chips with a little bit of oil (Optional), transfer the content to a airfryer and cook for 10 minutes at 360 degrees F.
3. Once done, sprinkle salt and pepper to taste. Store them in a Jar and serve as a snack.

Vegetarian Seek Kebab

Serves: 4
Prep time: 15 mins
Cook time: 10 mins
Total time: 25 mins

Ingredients

1 cup mixed vegetables, chopped

1/2 cup paneer

2 Medium boiled mashed potatoes

3 Green chillies

1 inch ginger

3-4 garlic cloves

1/4 cup fresh mint leaves

2 tbsp corn flour

1/2 tsp garam masala powder

Salt to taste

1 tbsp chaat masala

Oil for brushing

12-14 bamboo skewers

Instructions

1. Place the chopped vegetables, ginger, garlic, green chillies, mint leaves and paneer in a food processor and mince them.

2. In a large mixing bowl, add minced vegetables, mashed potatoes, garam masala powder, salt and cornflour. Mix well.

3. Once the kebab mixture is ready, divide equally into lemon sized balls (approximately 12 to 14). Wet your palms and shape each of them around individual bamboo skewers. Ensure that you press the ends firmly, so that they don't fall apart. Remember to soak the bamboo skewers in water for

at least 2-3 hours before using them or they will tend to burn.

4. Pre heat the Airfryer at 420 degrees F. Brush the kebabs with oil and air fry at 360 degrees F for 10 minutes or till slightly golden brown on the outside.

Mozzarella Sticks

Servings: 4
Prep time: 2 hours
Cook time: 12 mins
Total time: 2 hours 12 mins

Ingredients

1 lb Mozzarella cheese

2 Eggs

3 tbp Milk, nonfat

¼ cup White flour

1 cup Bread crumbs

Instructions

1. Cut cheese into 3 x 1/2 inch sticks.
2. Place bread crumbs in one bowl. Mix the egg and milk together in another bowl and set it aside.
3. Dip cheese sticks in the egg, and then in bread crumbs.
4. Lay breaded sticks on a cookie sheet.
5. Freeze in freezer for 1-2 hours or until solid.
6. Place small batches of breaded sticks (do not overcrowd) into the Fry Basket.
7. Cook in airfryer for 12 minutes at 400 degrees F.

Hot wings

Serves: 4
Prep time: 5 mins
Cook time: 30 mins
Total time: 35 mins

Ingredients

4lbs Chicken Wing Sections

½ cup Cayenne Pepper Sauce

½ cup Butter

1 tbp Worstershire Sauce

1-2 Tablespoons Light Brown Sugar

1 tsp Kosher Salt

Instructions

1. Place chicken wings in Air Fryer basket.

2. Cook at 380 degrees F for 25 minutes, shaking the basket half way through.

3. In a mixing cup, whisk together pepper sauce, butter, Worstershire, brown sugar and salt.

4. When Beep sounds, shake the wings, change temperature to 400 degrees F and cook 5 minutes more.

5. Remove wings from Air Fryer and dump into large mixing bowl. Add sauce and toss to mix.

Sweet Potato Fries

Serves: 1
Prep time: 5 mins
Cook time: 10 mins
Total time: 15 mins

Ingredients

1 Sweet potato

½ tsp coarse salt

½ tsp black pepper

½ Plum powder

Instructions

1. Scrub your sweet potato clean of dirt and chop into thin fries, roughly the same as conventional French fries found at a restaurant.
2. Place your fries into a bowl and mix in 1 tsp of cooking oil.
3. Place your fries into the airfryer to cook for 10 minutes at 360 degrees F or until cooked.
4. Mix the salt, pepper and plum powder together and season your fries before serving.

Note:

Plum powder can be found in most Asian supermarkets.

Healthy homemade potato chips

Serves: 2
Prep time: 15 mins
Cook time: 20 mins
Total time: 35 mins

Ingredients

2 large potatoes

Vegetable or olive oil in a spray bottle

Sea salt and freshly ground black pepper

Instructions

½ cup sour cream

1 tablespoon olive oil

2 scallions, white part only minced

¼ teaspoon salt

Freshly ground black pepper

¼ tsp lemon juice

Instructions

1. Wash the potatoes well, but leave the skins on. Slice them into ⅛-inch thin slices, using a mandolin or food processor. Rinse the potatoes under cold water until the water runs clear and then let them soak in a bowl of cold water for at least 10 minutes. Drain and dry the potato slices really well in a single layer on a clean kitchen towel.

2. Pre-heat the air fryer to 300 F. Spray the potato chips with the oil so that both sides are evenly coated, or rub the slices between your hands with some oil if you don't have a spray bottle.

3. Air-fry in two batches at 300 F for 15 to 20 minutes, shaking the basket a few times during the cooking process to move the chips

around so they cook more evenly. Season the finished chips with sea salt and freshly ground black pepper while they are still hot.

4.   While the chips are air-frying, make the sour cream and onion dip by mixing together the sour cream, olive oil, scallions, salt, pepper and lemon juice. Serve the chips warm or room temperature along with the dip.

Onion Rings

Serves: 3
Prep time: 5 mins
Cook time: 10 mins
Total time: 15 mins

Ingredient

1 large onion, cut into 1/4 inch slices
1 1/4 cups all purpose flour
1 tsp baking powder
1 tsp salt
1 egg
1 cup milk
3/4 cup dry bread crumbs

Instructions

1. Pre-heat the Air Fryer for about 10 minutes.

2. Separate onion slices into rings.

3. Mix together flour, baking powder and salt in a small bowl.

4. Dip onion slices into flour mixture until they are all coated. Set aside. Whisk egg and milk into flour using a fork. Dip the floured onion rings into the batter to coat.

5. Spread bread crumbs on a plate or shallow dish and dredge the rings into the crumbs, making sure it's all covered.

6. Place all the onion rings into Air Fryer and cook for 7-10 minutes at 360F, you can pop it open to check for doneness.

Prawn Toast

Serves: 2
Prep time: 10 mins
Cook time: 5 mins
Total time: 15 mins

Ingredients

500g Green king prawns, peeled and cleaned

2 Garlic cloves, finely chopped

½ Knob of ginger, peeled, finely chopped

1 tsp White sugar1eggwhite

1 tsp Sesame oil

4 Green onions, finely chopped

5 Slices stale white bread, crusts removed

1 Egg, lightly beaten

1 cup Japanese panko crumbs

Instructions

1. Put the prawns, garlic, ginger, sugar, egg white, sesame oil and ½ tsp sea salt in a food processor and process until smooth.
2. Put the mixture in a bowl and stir in the green onion.
3. Spread about 2 tbsp of the prawn mixture to the edges of each piece of bread and cut each in half diagonally.
4. Brush tops and sides of each piece with beaten egg, then press into breadcrumbs to coat.
5. Preheat airfryer to 360 degrees F.
6. Cook your prawn toast until breadcrumbs turn golden. (Approx 5 mins)

Potato Wedges

Serves: 1
Prep time: 40 mins
Cook time: 15 mins
Total time: 55 mins

Ingredients

1 Medium potato

1 tbsp Cooking oil

Dashes of paprika

Instructions

1. Scrub the potatoes clean and cut it into wedges. Soak the potato wedges in water for at least 30 minutes. Drain and pat dry with kitchen paper.

2. Coat them with oil in a bowl. Sprinkle with paprika powder.

3. Cook in airfryer for 15 minutes under 360 degrees F.

Cheese Toast

Serves: 1
Prep time: 5 mins
Cook time: 5 mins
Total time: 10 mins

Ingredients

1 slice of bread

60 g Grated cheddar cheese

10g Mozzarella

Instructions

1. Toast the bread in the toaster
2. Cover the toast with the cheese
3. Place in the airfryer at 200 degrees F for 5 minutes

Popcorn Chicken

Serves: 2
Prep time: 40 mins
Cook time: 15 mins
Total time: 55 mins

Ingredients

700 gr Boneless chicken breasts

1/2 tbsp Cooking wine

1/2 tbsp Soy souce

1 tsp 5 Spices powder

1/2 tsp Garlic powder

1/2 tsp Minced ginger

1/2 tsp Chilli powder

1/4 tsp Pepper powder

1/2 tsp Salt

1 pack Tapioca starch

Instructions

1. Cut the chicken into small chunks. Place in a large bowl.

2. Add all ingredients into the bowl except tapioca powder, and mix it up.

3. Marinate the chicken chunks for about 10 minutes.

4. Place half of the tapioca starch in the large bowl and ensure all chicken pieces are coated.

5. Once the powdered process done, cover the plate with plastic film. Put the chicken chunks into the fridge. Leave it around 30 minutes.

6. Remove the chicken from the fridge and use the rest of the tapioca flour to coat the chicken once more.

7. Cook in airfryer at 360 degree F. for 15 minutes or until fully cooked depending on size of your chicken chunks

DESSERT RECIPES

Apple Pie

Serves: 4
Prep time: 5 mins
Cook time: 15 mins
Total time: 20 mins

Ingredients

3 Small apples chopped or finely sliced

2 tbsp Brown sugar

1tsps Cinnamon

¼ tsp Nutmeg

1 tbsp All purpose flour

2 Sheets of thawed filo pastry

¼ cup melted butter

Instructions

1. Place your chopped apples, brown sugar, cinnamon and nutmeg into a bowl. Mix all the ingredients thoroughly.

2. Take 4 ramekin dishes and fill them with your apple pie filling.

3. Roll out both filo pastry sheets and cut both sheets in half.

4. Brush the rims of your ramekin dishes with melted butter and place a filo pastry sheet on top. The excess trimmings around the edge should be tucked inside the dish.

5. Brush the surface of the filo pastry with melted butter.

6. Place your apple pies into the air fryer for 10 – 15 minutes at 360 F. Check on them every 5 minutes.

Note:

The smaller you chop the apples the softer and more caramelize your apple pies filling will be.

Chocolate Lava Cake

Serves: 2
Prep time: 10 mins
Cook time: 3 mins
Total time: 13 mins

Ingredients

150g Melted cooking chocolate

150g Butter

75g Sugar

2 Eggs

80g Plain flour

Salt to taste

Instructions

1. With a food processor, mix the butter and sugar until butter is softened. Add in the egg and bend until the mixture is creamy.

2. With a spatula, pour the mixture into a mixing bowl and stir in the salt, flour and melted chocolate. Blend the ingredients thoroughly.

3. Preheat the air fryer to 360 F.

4. Grease two ramekin dishes and sprinkle a layer of sugar within the interior of the dishes.

5. Pour in the cake mixture into each dish and allow to cook for 3 minutes in the air fryer.

Note:

You'll want to keep a close eye on the cake to ensure the lava middle doesn't get over cooked.

Coffee Cake

Serves: 4
Prep time: 10 mins
Cook time: 25 mins
Total time: 35 mins

Ingredients

50g Soft butter

50g Caster sugar

1 Egg

70g Plain flour

1 tbp Cocoa

1/2 cup of instant coffee

Salt to taste

50g Dark chocolate

Instructions

1. Preheat the air fryer to 320 F

2. In a food processor, beat the butter and sugar until light and creamy. Then add the egg, and allow that to blend into the butter.

3. Add the flour, cocoa powder, coffee and salt to the mixture and mix well with a spatula.

4. Pour in the dark chocolate chunks before pouring the entire mixture into a greased baking pan.

5. Place the baking pan into the air fryer to cook for 25 minutes, or until done.

Note:

Check if your cake is done by sticking a knife into it. If the knife comes out clean then your cake is done.

Fudge Brownies

Serves: 10
Prep time: 15 mins
Cook time: 20 mins
Total time: 35 mins

Ingredients

75g Cooking chocolate

75g Butter

1 Large egg

60g Sugar

1tsp Vanilla essence

Salt to taste

40g Self-raising flour

25g Walnuts chopped

Instructions

1. Melt the butter and chocolate together on low heat by stirring continuously. Set the mixture aside to cool to room temperature.

2. Preheat the air fryer to 360 F.

3. Beat the egg in a bowl with the sugar, vanilla essence and a pinch of salt until light and creamy. Beat in the chocolate mixture well, and then stir in the self-raising four and walnuts.

4. Grease the baking pan and then pour your brownie mix in.

5. Place the baking pan into the air fryer to cook for 20 minutes. Check on it every 5 minutes after the first 10 minutes has passed to ensure the middle is still soft and moist but the top is crispy.

Chocolate profiteroles

Serves: 9
Prep time: 10 mins
Cook time: 10 mins
Total time: 20 mins

Ingredients

100g Butter

200g Plain flour

6 Medium eggs

300ml water

Whipped cream

Chocolate sauce

Instructions

1. Preheat the air fryer to 340 F

2. Place the butter in the water in a large pan and cook on a medium to low heat until melted and well combined.

3. Remove it from the heat and stir in the flour (a bit at a time) and then put it back on the heat until it forms a big dough in the middle of the pan.

4. Set the dough to one side so that it can cool down. Add in the eggs and mix well until you have a smooth textured dough.

5. Make into profiterole shapes and cook for 10 minutes on 180c.

6. Once done, allow the profiteroles to cool before cutting them into halves and filling them with whipped cream.

7. Finish your profiteroles with melted chocolate on top.

Note:

You can set the chocolate by placing them into the refrigerator before serving.

COOKING CONVERSION CHART

Measurement

CUP	ONCES	MILLILITERS	TABLESPOONS
8 cup	64 oz	1895 ml	128
6 cup	48 oz	1420 ml	96
5 cup	40 oz	1180 ml	80
4 cup	32 oz	960 ml	64
2 cup	16 oz	480 ml	32
1 cup	8 oz	240 ml	16
3/4 cup	6 oz	177 ml	12
2/3 cup	5 oz	158 ml	11
1/2 cup	4 oz	118 ml	8
3/8 cup	3 oz	90 ml	6
1/3 cup	2.5 oz	79 ml	5.5
1/4 cup	2 oz	59 ml	4
1/8 cup	1 oz	30 ml	3
1/16 cup	1/2 oz	15 ml	1

Temperature

FAHRENHEIT	CELSIUS
100 °F	37 °C
150 °F	65 °C
200 °F	93 °C
250 °F	121 °C
300 °F	150 °C
325 °F	160 °C
350 °F	180 °C
375 °F	190 °C
400 °F	200 °C
425 °F	220 °C
450 °F	230 °C
500 °F	260 °C
525 °F	274 °C
550 °F	288 °C

Weight

IMPERIAL	METRIC
1/2 oz	15 g
1 oz	29 g
2 oz	57 g
3 oz	85 g
4 oz	113 g
5 oz	141 g
6 oz	170 g
8 oz	227 g
10 oz	283 g
12 oz	340 g
13 oz	369 g
14 oz	397 g
15 oz	425 g
1 lb	453 g

Made in the USA
Coppell, TX
02 December 2019